Pursuing Freedom

PURSUING FREEDOM

BECOMING THE MAN YOU COULD BE

THOMAS WURTZ

Our Sunday Visitor
Huntington, Indiana

Our Sunday Visitor Publishing Division
Our Sunday Visitor, Inc.
200 Noll Plaza
Huntington, IN 46750
www.osv.com
1-800-348-2440

ISBN: 978-1-68192-348-2 (Inventory No. T2034)
1. SELF-HELP—Personal Growth—General.
2. RELIGION—Christianity—Saints & Sainthood.
3. RELIGION—Christianity—Catholic.

eISBN: 978-1-68192-349-9
LCCN: 2020933200

Cover design: Tyler Ottinger
Cover art: Adobe Stock
Interior design: Lindsey Riesen

PRINTED IN THE UNITED STATES OF AMERICA

To my children: Louis, Bruno, Margaret, Rocco, and Cecilia. Thank you for challenging me to become the man God wants me to be. And to my wife, Kate, for loving me on the journey.

Contents

Contents

Introduction

My two boys are sitting at the kitchen table with me as I write. One is eating paper. The other is working on reading three-letter words with my wife. As I look at them, I am reminded of a few things. First, DNA is fascinating — both of my boys are blond and fair-skinned, while I am neither of those things. And second, I am reminded of how much weight I carry as a father raising sons. I will be for my boys the primary example of what it means to be a man. That is an exhilarating but potentially overwhelming thought. Our lived experience of masculinity is often all over the spectrum, especially in our modern culture, which doesn't want to admit that there is a difference between masculine and feminine.

As a young man, I wanted nothing more than to become what a man is supposed to be. The problem was, I had little idea of what that really meant, and not enough men were pointing me in the right direction. I developed physical strength and certain freedoms to do what I wanted — to taste what the world had to serve me. I had a decent amount going for me: good grades, athletic prowess, a stable family environment, and Air Jordans. I was a young man aimlessly exploring the concepts of masculinity and being a man. Like many men today, I did not immediately realize I was lost. The moment I did realize it was a moment of intense anguish. When I finally vomited up the lies the world fed me, I was eager to find the right path. The heroes of history books and movies always spoke straight to my heart as a man. I realized there was more to manhood than the life I had been living. At the same time, I didn't know how to proceed. My freedom, my strength — what should I do with these things?

I know that this story resonates with many other men — a story of uncertainty and failure. I see too many grown men walking around as if they were half dead. I know how that feels; I was once that way.

While many of us, along with our culture, might be wandering aimlessly, we do not have to be. We have a clear path for our lives as Christian men. This path begins and ends in Jesus Christ. He is the model, the teacher, and the one who will move us down that path. This path has the capacity to change the world. As Archbishop Chaput wrote,

> It's a good thing, a vital thing, to consider what we're willing to die for. What do we love more than life? To even ask that question is an act of rebellion against a loveless age. And to answer it with conviction is to become a revolutionary; the kind of loving revolutionary who will survive and resist — and someday redeem a late modern West that can no longer imagine anything worth dying for, and thus, in the long run, anything worth living for.[1]

Not only does our call as men give us something profound to die for; it also clearly gives us something worthwhile to live for. Once we understand why God made us in a particular way as men, we can lay out a path to flourish within that plan. I hope that this book, along with others, can help each of us to realize what it means to flourish as God intends and desires us to do.

A good place to start in understanding that reality is in the very beginning.

CHAPTER 1
Guard and Protect

The purpose in a man's mind is like deep water,
but a man of understanding will draw it out.
Proverbs 20:5

•••

Faith means battles; if there are no contests, it is because
there are none who desire to contend.
Saint Ambrose

When I was in seventh grade, my teacher walked over to my desk as the class was busy working. She was impressed that I had opened a textbook to seek an answer to her classroom question. This move prompted immediate affirmation. As she bent down and made eye contact, she asked, "What do you want to do when you get older?" I didn't have to think about this at all — I knew the answer. "Be a basketball player," I responded.

These conversations happen every day, and it's a good thing to encourage young people to have aspirations for their lives. For young men today, however, this is becoming a more interesting conversation. As fewer of us go to college[2] and more of us seem to be living at home, drifting,[3] I wonder if we have forgotten to help one another learn the deeper mission innate to the male sex. Understanding this mission might help men today to find the purpose many have either not found or have stopped looking for because they got tired of seeking.

The truth is, God knows us, and he designed us in a particular way as men. We are made in his image and likeness. Genesis 2:15 tells us that after God made man, he ordered him to "till and keep" the Garden. The Hebrew word translated here as "keep" is *shamar*. I never really understood why God was so keen on having Adam keep the Garden tidy. Then someone told me a different way to understand *shamar*. While "keep" is one way to translate this Hebrew word, another is "to guard and/or protect."[4] I think this provides a fuller context — God is giving Adam basic instructions on his mission and task. It also helps us understand the significance of our masculinity and why God so clearly tasked Adam with doing this important work in the Garden.[5] God was ordering the first man to guard, to protect, and to fight (if need be) to keep all of creation in right order. The Garden was perfect. It didn't yet know sin, and Adam, as God's son, was meant to participate in an intimate way in preserving it. You can picture this command being given with some background drumbeat, and Adam clenching his fists as he surveys the Garden, similar to a football player ready to run down the field on a kickoff. I think this reality — this call to *shamar* — has been stamped on every man's soul. It is part of why we fight, why we love to compete, and why we "worship" great athletes and military heroes. It is why my five-year-old son asks every day if we can fight, and why my two-year-old boy does his best to join us.

This call to shamar has been stamped on every man's soul.

Many of us are familiar with the story in the next chapter of Genesis: The serpent tempts Eve to eat the fruit, and both she and Adam do so. Thus, sin enters the world. The question we have to ask here is: Where was Adam in his *shamaring* duties? He seems to have failed miserably in his task to guard and protect. In fact, this failure of Adam changed the course of salvation history. Adam and Eve didn't trust God's goodness and failed to live his command. Their decision not only brought original sin upon all of us; it also got them kicked out of the Garden. And, as they left, God placed an angel with a flaming sword to *shamar* the entrance into the Garden (see Gn 3:24) so

Adam and Eve couldn't sneak back in.

God, in his goodness, would take up where Adam failed. As Saint Paul writes in Romans 5:18, "as one man's trespass led to condemnation for all men, so one man's act of righteousness leads to acquittal and life for all men." Jesus becomes the New Adam. He fulfills the original task of Adam and saves what Adam broke. As our Savior, Jesus invites each of us uniquely to take part in the same call to *shamar* that he took up in Adam's stead.

If we stop to think about this concept of guarding and protecting, we should feel an adrenaline rush of sorts. Or maybe, as I often do, we begin to daydream about being a hero. We might ponder why God gave us men this responsibility to *shamar*. What exactly are we guarding and protecting now that we aren't in the Garden of Eden anymore? And what are we guarding it from? I think the Bible answers this by pointing to two things.

First, what are we guarding? To answer, let's look at two moments in the life and ministry of Jesus, beginning with the Gospel of John, chapter 18. Jesus Christ has been arrested and handed over to the local Roman authority, Pontius Pilate. Pilate questions Jesus about who he is and what his mission entails. They go back and forth, and then Jesus unloads, in typical form, this hit: "For this I was born, and for this I have come into the world, to bear witness to the truth. Everyone who is of the truth hears my voice" (v. 37). Jesus names a significant aspect of his mission, which is to show us truth. If Jesus himself came to bear witness to truth, then part of our duty as sons of God is to protect and guard truth.

A second scriptural event that gives insight into this question of what men are called to *shamar* is found in Matthew 22:36, where Jesus is asked about the greatest commandment. His response? "You shall love the Lord your God with all your heart, and with all your soul, and with all your mind. This is the great and first commandment. And a second is like it, You shall love your neighbor as yourself" (Mt 22:37–39). He couldn't be more crystal clear: Love is our aim, and truth is our guide. Really, it is rather simple: As men, we are tasked with guarding and protecting, to the point of laying down our lives, the mission of Christ. This mission includes the pursuit of charity and truth and ultimately will transform us more and more into the image of Jesus Christ. As such, charity is our calling — all our actions and thoughts should be directed to this with Jesus on the cross as the incarnate image of this love. Truth is what inspires and guides our living of charity; it helps us discern what love is in each moment of our lives. We, as men, are meant to protect the dissemination of this vision of life, again, in imitation of our Lord.

Second, from what (or whom) are we to guard and protect this mission of Christ?

To answer this question, we should again look to Christ. Saint John writes in his first letter, "The reason the Son of God appeared was to destroy the works of the devil" (1 Jn 3:8). Our task begins by guarding against the devil and his minions as they seek to destroy truth and love and the souls of all people. As Adam dwelt in the Garden of Eden ready to defend it and his bride, so should we. Anything — any concept, person, government, etc. — that seeks to destroy truth and love must be guarded against, lest it pervert the nature and order of God's creation. We should exercise our call to *shamar* in many ways, even our modern daily lives. But we are called to *shamar* first within our families and spheres of influence. As a husband and father, my first duty is to my wife and children, then to the society in which God has placed me. The examples of ways to exercise this call are endless. Here are some from my life:

- In the checkout line at the grocery store, I often flip over the magazines that are too sexual for my young children and replace them in the rack backward.
- I canceled our Netflix account when Netflix threatened the state of Georgia due to its pro-life laws and when I learned of Netflix's financial support of Planned Parenthood.
- I pray with my children each night.
- I try to engage in debates about public policy and vote in a manner that reflects Judeo-Christian truths. I especially seek to support ending abortion in any way I can.
- I don't put myself in situations that would harm the integrity of my marriage.

All of this is easier said than done, as we men know all too well. We like a lot of things, and we are drawn to various pleasures and comforts, many of them directly harmful to our physical, mental, and spiritual health. We become mesmerized by the culture around us and forget what helps us and what hurts us. There are many forces, both internal and external, seeking to reduce our effectiveness to *shamar* properly. Like handcuffs, they restrict us. Because of this, if we want to live out our call to *shamar*, we have to live lives of true freedom. This freedom is part of our innate dignity as human persons, and it is not simply freedom to do whatever we want whenever we want — a very problematic under-standing of freedom. True freedom is the freedom to exist as we were made to exist. This freedom gives us the ability to respond to our duty to guard and protect as the Lord calls us.

What does this freedom look like? Consider some examples: An athlete who isn't free won't be able to take the shot or make the tackle. A soldier who isn't free won't be able to engage the enemy effectively, if at all. So it is for us as men: When we are not free, we are incapable of doing what God wants us to do. Another way to say this: We are enslaved.

So how do we become free? My hope with this book is to provide some guidance that will help men begin to work toward finding the freedom necessary to *shamar* — to become fully alive as men. This book comes from years of strug-gling, failing, and growing in my life. Perhaps even more importantly, it comes from studying the lives of great saints who clearly exemplified what it means to be a man and to live out God's call to *shamar*. This book will explore eight key areas that men in our culture need to focus on. These areas will allow us more fully to live in freedom and to ful-fill our duty to *shamar*. We will also look at the examples of eight great saints who illustrated these various aspects of the call to *shamar* in heroic and incredible ways.

We were made in God's image and likeness with an im-mense role to play in serving humanity, yet our current male culture is dominated by mediocrity and confusion. As a cul-ture, we have forgotten what it means to be men. Yet, in two decades of leading, shaping, and aiding in the formation of young men, I have seen that men today have a tremendous capacity to respond and become who God wants us to be-come. And in Jesus and his saints, we also have the example and help of men who have taught us what we need in order to thrive. When we seek to imitate them, we will find the freedom to live as the images of God we were created to be. We will become more fully the men God designed us to be, and we will be able to make the world more of what God desires for it.

Men today have a tremendous capacity to respond and become who God wants us to become.

As you work through this book, let the lives of the saints inspire you. Allow each chapter to build on that inspiration while both informing you and causing you to reflect on your life.

If we embrace the reality of who we were created to be and live properly within it, we can transform the culture, the world, our families. And, by God's grace, we will see our own souls and the souls around us be restored.

CHAPTER 2

Engage in the Battle
Around Us

The life of man upon earth is a warfare.
Job 7:1, Douay-Rheims

•••

The devil flatters that he may deceive us; he charms that he may injure us; he allures that he may slay us.
Saint John Climacus

Whether we realize it or not, we are engaged in a war. At every moment of every day, demonic spirits seek to wreak havoc on our world and on our souls. The Devil and his minions never stop, never rest, and they hate us. As Saint Peter warns us, "Be sober, be watchful. Your adversary the devil prowls around like a roaring lion, seeking someone to devour" (1 Pt 5:8). Many in our day and age doubt that the Devil is real, much less a threat to our souls. This doubt does not stop the work of demons, however; it gives them strength. Above all, they want us to minimize the threat in our minds, to think that demons really aren't that big a deal for us to be concerned about. The more they can make us apathetic toward them, the more power they gain over us.

If we honestly assess our current culture in the West, it seems clear that the Devil is succeeding in his strategy. This should enrage us, since we have been charged with guarding and protecting our loved ones and the whole of society. As a dear friend of mine said, "It is a *real war*. People die, and they die *forever*. People are born again, and they live *forever*." The Devil is working ceaselessly to make sure as many people as possible die forever and burn with him in hell. This is a sobering thought, and it's one we can't shy away from if we are serious in our pursuit of freedom. In reality, our pursuit of freedom has eternal ramifications, not just for us, but for the whole world. And the pursuit begins with acknowledging that this spiritual warfare is the reality we live in.

In this is our first challenge to freedom, and hence, our first challenge to *shamar* effectively. The Devil desires to pull as many souls to hell as he possibly can. If we fail to recognize this spiritual battle raging around us for our souls and every other soul, we will fail to respond to it. We are engaged in a great war, whether we like it or not. And like all wars, we can choose to spend our lives for the cause of victory, or we can be crushed. What should *not* be an option is *not* to fight. This war, which is the result of man's choice to sin, beginning with the first sin of Adam and Eve in the Garden of Eden, impacts each and every one of us. We step into it upon our birth. It contains infinitely more dangers than the stories we read in books and the movies we watch. As we navigate the battlefield day by day, we find it riddled with temptation, deception, and doubt. It can be tempting to disengage, to step off to the sidelines and hope it will all blow over without our effort. Yet this is not possible. The moment we cease to fight, we fall prey to the Devil, who prowls like a roaring lion looking for someone to devour. He is seeking to distract us, divide us, and kill any faith we may have. He hates us and wants to enslave us so that we will no longer be capable of living our call as men. If we hope to *shamar*, we must step into this battle.

In reality, our pursuit of freedom has eternal ramifications, not just for us, but for the whole world.

Saint Pio of Pietrelcina

In 1968, an old Capuchin friar in a small town in Italy died. Saint Pio (better known as Padre Pio) spent his entire life in a direct battle with the Devil. For him, this was not just a spiritual reality but a physical one as well. He knew that the Christian is always embroiled in a war against Satan and his minions. Padre Pio's encounters with Satan were direct and frequent. As a result, his life was constantly in tune with the spiritual world and the battle against sin and Satan.

Padre Pio never retreated from the battle. He loved Jesus intimately and desired all souls to be freed from the grip of sin and Satan so that they might receive the love of our heavenly Father and give themselves in love back to him. Padre Pio is a model for us in the spiritual battle, because he experienced the strength and terror of the Devil firsthand, yet he bravely refused to be a passive casualty. Just as a soldier goes off to fight for the country and people he loves, so Padre Pio fought because of his love for God and souls.

Padre Pio was born on May 25, 1887, in Pietrelcina, Italy. From an early age, he experienced visions and direct encounters with the spiritual world. It happened so frequently that, when he was young, he supposed this was everyone's normal experience. As one biographer describes it:

> From the age of five, he was not only very sensitive about matters pertaining to God, but began having visions of spirits, at times very beautiful ones, and at times very ugly ones. It was the horrible visions that scared him and caused him to cry. … The child was in no position to appreciate the extraordinary character of these phenomena and diabolic interventions. He did not speak of them to anyone and considered such events to be ordinary occurrences in everyone's life. At that early age he was well aware that life has to do with two realms of opposing realities; which are, on the one hand, the reality

of God and of heaven, and on the other hand the
reality of the devil and of things that are sinful leading to eternal separation from God. He committed
himself entirely to God's side.[6]

Padre Pio's encounters with the spiritual world only in-
creased in intensity as he grew older. God gave him a number
of graces and gifts that elevated his holiness and extended
his impact on those around him. Because of this, the enemy
knew that his typical efforts to draw souls to himself would
not work on Padre Pio. Instead, all the Devil could do was
attack him, sometimes with physical abuse.

The Devil's attacks intensified after Padre Pio was ordained on August 10, 1910. The Devil appeared to him in
vile forms, such as black, filthy animals and provocative
women. Sometimes the Devil would spit in Padre Pio's face
or haunt him with deafening sounds. At other times, he
would appear to Padre Pio in more attractive forms: as an
angel of light, as our crucified Lord, as the father superior of
his order, as Saint Pius X, Saint Francis of Assisi, Our Lady,
and even the saint's guardian angel. Padre Pio was exhausted by the constant assault of Satan, but he persevered at every moment, knowing that Our Lord had already won the
war against his enemy, and that God's grace would see him
through. He wrote, "The field of battle between God and
Satan is the human soul. This is where it takes place every
moment of our lives. The soul must give free access to our
Lord and be completely fortified by him with every kind of
weapon. His light must illumine it to fight the darkness of
error; he must put on Jesus Christ, his truth and justice, the
shield of faith, the word of God to overcome such powerful
enemies. To put on Jesus Christ, we must die to ourselves."[7]

• • •

Like Padre Pio, you and I must wake up every morning and choose. We can choose to enter the battle (by doing the good, no matter what the cost to us), or we can choose to passively watch life pass us by. Herein lies our calling to become the men God made us to be. Each of us daily experiences the "unseen and inner struggle, which every Christian undertakes from the moment of his baptism, when he makes a vow to God to fight for Him, to the glory of His divine Name, even unto death."[8] We stand as warriors under the command of our Lord Jesus Christ, strengthened by his grace for the fight in which we must engage. The war is not an option — but to be a casualty is.

This is the good news of our call as Christians: The war is not the end; it is merely a step toward our ultimate goal in life — to be with God in heaven. War is not for its own sake. In the end, we hope to find peace; we hope to find love; we hope to find the Person of Jesus Christ. Just think of the movie *Saving Private Ryan*. The small band of soldiers engage in a number of battles, avoiding death and injury, all for the sake of their end — to bring Private Ryan back home. They were not fighting simply for the sake of fighting; they were fighting for a mission, and in a much bigger way, so are we.

> *The war is not an option — but to be a casualty is.*

Our call to *shamar* — the same call embraced by countless holy men throughout salvation history — is a call to give all for love of Christ and love of others. When we opt out of the fight, we abandon this incredible call. We say no to the lonely neighbor in need of a visit. We say no to the public discourse seeking to defend human dignity. We say no to eradicating the junk from our lives — and instead, we live life staring at a screen. Our habits of laziness, disengagement, and sin make us weak, and it becomes harder and harder for us to step into the fight. We can so easily become entangled in the snares of sin that to love as Christ calls us to love becomes nearly impossible, because we lack the freedom to give. Instead, we run around in circles, caught in the trap of our self-love, unable to give without counting the cost.

A man who refuses to fight this spiritual battle becomes a man who is not free. Of course, fighting is not our ultimate purpose in life; our purpose is to love and be with God for all eternity. But we cannot achieve that ultimate purpose, or help others to do so, if we are not free. When we decide not to engage in the fight, we give up on freedom and submit to slavery. When we refuse to fight, we automatically lose. There is no middle ground. We become imprisoned by sin, Satan, and ultimately death. We have two choices in this matter, and both boil down to what we hope to do for all eternity: Do we want to love God selflessly or love ourselves selfishly? This question has only two possible answers, and the way we choose has eternal consequences.

If we want to step into our call to *shamar* and engage in the war that confronts us, we have to wake up to the reality of the spiritual battle that surrounds us. We can't hide from it. Instead, let us plant our flag with Christ and do everything we can to engage in this war. As one spiritual writer encourages us:

> Do not, therefore, lose heart, although you may think it is a difficult task to absorb the attacks of so many enemies, that this warfare will continue your

entire lifetime, and that inescapable ruin threatens you on all sides. But remember this — neither the power nor the trickery of your enemies can hurt you without the permission of Him for Whose honor you fight. He delights in this kind of battle and, as far as possible, encourages everyone to engage in it. But He is so far from permitting your enemies to accomplish their evil plans that He will fight on your side and sooner or later crown your endeavors with victory, though the battle may end only with your life.[9]

Unless we are willing to fight, we cannot live our call to guard and protect the mission of Christ. We must recognize our enemy in his attacks and his clever disguises. To do otherwise is to surrender. As Padre Pio reminds us, the Devil is looking for someone to devour — but we do not have to be afraid. When we are united to Christ and willing to stand in the fray, the enemy will retreat.

The enemy is smart. He is also mad, because, in the end, he knows he has lost. But he wants to take as many of us down with him as he can. Here are some things you can start to put into practice to make this more difficult for him:

- Stay away from anything that claims to conjure spirits and anything connected to the occult. Also avoid seeking hidden knowledge apart from God. (I suggest you avoid even the Magic 8-Ball.)
- Stay close to Jesus by talking with him daily. Read the Bible often.
- Remain connected to God's grace by at-

tending Mass weekly, going to confession regularly (once a month is often recommended), and avoiding sin, especially serious sin (the Church refers to this as mortal sin).

- The Devil and his demons can manipulate our imagination, and they know what we have seen. For this reason, try to consume only media (TV, movies, music, books, and so forth) that glorifies God.
- Develop a relationship with Mary.
- Imitate the life of Jesus Christ.

Finally, pray these prayers that are powerful for protection in the spiritual battle:

- the Our Father (the last petition arms us against the power of evil)
- Psalm 91 (a very powerful prayer for protection)
- the Hail Mary (Mary is the Devil's worst nightmare)

CHAPTER 3

Control Our Passions

A fool gives full vent to his anger,
but a wise man quietly holds it back.
Proverbs 29:11

• • •

A man who governs his passions is master of the world. We
must either command them or be enslaved by them.
Saint Dominic

Every day we feel. We can't avoid it. We feel fear, sadness, anger, awe, and joy, among dozens of other feelings. Sometimes we might just feel numb.

Our feelings can be powerful — irresistible even. While feelings are neither good nor bad in themselves, they can be powerful influences on our actions, for good or for evil. The *Catechism of the Catholic Church* states: "The human person is ordered to beatitude by his deliberate acts: the passions or feelings he experiences can dispose him to it and contribute to it" (1762). When rightly ordered, our passions can drive us to acts of great virtue, but if we let strong feelings get the better of us, they can also lead us into sin. Each of us has our own struggle when it comes to controlling our passions. This struggle can be debilitating when it overpowers our ability to think clearly and choose wisely. Yet part of our call as Christian men is to ensure that our heads always lead the charge and put our passions in the place of serving rather than controlling.

Before we can engage effectively in the battle before us to be who God intends us to be, we need to focus inward so that we can allow the light and grace of Christ to heal us and help us function as God desires. Too often, our passions are left unchecked and take us out at the knees. Just as it is hard to breathe with someone squeezing our throat, so is it hard to live when we become choked by our passions, unable to act in freedom. As men, we have many passions vying for control of our lives. In my experiences, the three that tend to impact men most negatively are anger, fear, and sexual desire.

When it's out of control, anger can cause us to act in various ways — from a complete rush of irrational action to a tendency to check out completely. Uncontrolled anger can become a serious issue, especially for men. Here are a few statistics that illustrate what happens when men do not govern their anger:

- One in seven women have been injured by an intimate partner.[10]
- In 2010, more than 77 percent of homicides in the United States were perpetrated by men.[11]
- In 2010, one in five women in the United States had been raped in her lifetime.[12]

While anger can have a proper place (picture Jesus over-turning the moneychangers' tables in the Temple), it too often gets out of control for us men. An out-of-control man is clearly unable to guard and protect truth in love.

Fear is an interesting emotion. Uncontrolled fear can manifest itself in behaviors that range from terror of failure (picture the workaholic) to refusal to engage in any situation that might hurt someone's feelings (think of the chronic "people pleaser"). In my life, fear of failure had been a constant struggle. I know this is the case for lots of other men as well. I also know what it is like to fear giving of myself to another — to put down something I enjoy doing to play with my kids after a long day, or to stop and listen to my wife talk about something on her mind. We fear that giving too much will hurt, even if that fear is subconscious. We fear that we can give only so much of ourselves.

James Stenson has a tremendous book called *Successful Fathers*. Toward the end of it, he lists the characteristics of a "successful father":

> Finally, the most successful fathers always put their family's welfare ahead of their jobs. They know that their children can be seriously hurt through father-ly neglect, and no job advantages — no raises or promotions or projects completed — can compen-sate for this loss.
>
> Sad to say, it's common for many men to reach late middle-age or retirement and find disappoint-ment in the results of their life's work ... but what about the children? They do endure forever, for their souls are immortal. The children's earthly and eternal happiness depends, in enormous mea-sure, on their father's influence during the first two decades of life. ... Parents have one chance — and only one — to raise their children right.[13]

Today's young fathers might be less likely than previous generations to be workaholics. They are more likely to come home on time to play video games and thus be just as distant as a dad who spends too many hours at the office. While the dad who overworks might fear coming in second or some-how failing in his job, the dad who tunes out at home can be just as damaging because he is afraid to give too much.

Uncontrolled sexual desire (or lust) can be more self-evident, but it isn't always. We live in a highly over-sexualized culture. Sex is everywhere. We might not even realize we are lusting after some half-naked woman, because half-naked women are everywhere. Lust has become normalized in our culture, to the point that we often don't recognize it. But one area where the problem is becoming increasingly evident is the plague of pornography. Most men today have seen or regularly look at pornography in some form. Many are addicted to it. This enslavement affects not only the men themselves, but the whole society, from the viewers' wives and families to the people (women and children) who are exploited in the creation of pornographic material.

We all like statistics. They can be enlightening, but I don't want to tempt us to turn our gaze outward at the general decline in sexual morality around us. I want this to speak to each of *us* directly. Still, we need to look at the statistics to get a sense of the broad scope of the problem we face:

- One out of three Americans seeks out porn at least once a month.[14]
- One in ten American males (ages thirteen and older) views porn daily.[15]
- Fewer than half (44 percent) of American males consider viewing pornography wrong.[16]
- "According to Shared Hope International's report on the demand for sex trafficking, use of pornography is the primary gateway to the purchase of humans for sex."[17]

While it is important for us to care about our neighbor and our depraved culture, we must first acknowledge our own struggles in this area. Chances are we are struggling with living a pure life. For some, it might be as small as ogling the gal who walks by. For others, it might be a complete addiction to pornography, an affair, or even the frequenting of strip clubs and other businesses that capitalize on our weakness.

Even if our skirmishes are with a different passion, it is our duty to discern the direction our passions might be leading us at any given moment and to be sure they are serving us, not command- ing us. Many of us are blind as a result of our passions dominating our lives. If we aren't yet blind, we have weak moments that restrict our capacity to think clearly and act properly. We often lose our freedom in these instances. When

It is our duty to discern the direction our passions might be leading us at any given moment and to be sure they are serving us, not commanding us.

this occurs, the duty to *shamar* is difficult to fulfill. A mag- nificent symphony, whether it be Mozart's or Haydn's, can help us to see the power of perfect harmony. The many in- struments, in order to play beautiful music, must play si- multaneously in harmonious perfection. Our passions are a little like those many instruments, and they need to be tem- pered so that we can exist in perfect harmony within our- selves.[18] Only then do our lives become a magnificent sym- phony. Only then are we free to live out our mission as men.

A Boss of a Man

If you have ever ventured around the Great Lakes region, you might have come across parishes and shrines dedicated to the North American Martyrs. These were eight French Jesuits who traveled that region, then known as New France, in the seventeenth century to bring the Gospel to the native peoples there. Saint Jean de Brébeuf was one of these eight men, and for years, he worked among the Hurons. His fellow missionaries hailed him as the outstanding missionary of all of New France. His religious superior wrote of him, "His evenness of temper seemed to be the virtue that outweighed all others. Nothing could upset him. During the twelve years I have known him, whether as superior or subject, I never saw him angry or even slightly indignant."[19] Among his many gifts, Father Brébeuf had extreme self-mastery. He governed his emotions and desires — not the other way around — and this made him highly effective in carrying out his God-given mission.

Standing well over six feet tall, he was a man impressive on the outside as well as on the inside. He was born on March 25, 1593, to a noble Normandy family, and at the age of twenty-four, he entered the Jesuit Order. He was a man of strict obedience and faithfulness to the Ignatian rule and spirit and was known to have asserted, "I will be ground to powder rather than break a rule."[20] He was ordained a priest on February 19, 1622.

When an appeal came to France for help in bringing the Gospel to the native peoples in North America, Father Brébeuf volunteered. Along with two other priests and two lay brothers, he set sail for Quebec on April 24, 1625. On July 25 of that year, Father Brébeuf accompanied a Huron party, which had come to Quebec for trading, back to their village. The Hurons found him admirable for his virtue, especially after seeing him travel in a canoe not big enough for a man of his stature. One biographer writes, "He had paddled his share, he was not sick, he had been invariably pleasant, and apparently had not rocked the boat. Seeing him pick up a heavy pack and carry it with back unbent over a long portage, the Hurons named him 'Echon,' meaning 'The-man-who-carries-the-load.' "[21]

He eventually arrived at the Huron village called Toanche. There he engaged in learning their language and examining their customs and beliefs. He learned quickly that the natives, though they formed strong family units to help raise children, were sexually promiscuous. They sought satisfaction for their sexual instincts with little decency or control — and they expected Father Brébeuf and his fellow Jesuit to do the same. The priests were often embarrassed by the way the Huron women pursued them and tempted them to marry them or have children with them.

Father Brébeuf and his companion had heroic virtue in the midst of this promiscuous environment. Brébeuf's confessor wrote: "(His chastity) was proof; and in that matter his eyes were so faithful to his heart that they had no sight for the objects which might have spoiled his purity. His body was not rebellious to the spirit; and in the midst of impurity itself — which reigns, it seems, in this country — he lived in an innocence as great as if he had sojourned in the midst of a desert inaccessible to that sin."[22]

In 1628, the French fort of Quebec finally surrendered to the English. One of the terms of the surrender was the expulsion of the Jesuits. As Father Brébeuf sailed away with his fellow Jesuits, leaving the land and people he was dedicated to serving, he had tears in his eyes. Eventually the French regained the region, however, and Father Brébeuf returned in May 1633.

Meanwhile, the Iroquois had been increasing their attacks on the Huron nation. In March 1649, St. Ignace, a Huron mission, was conquered by the Iroquois. They slaughtered everyone there and then made their way to St. Louis, where Father Brébeuf and another priest were finishing their prayers after Mass. Many fled the village, while a small number of warriors prepared a defense. Father Brébeuf and his fellow priest chose to stay and minister to their flock to the end. They were captured and tortured cruelly before dying heroic deaths. Only a man who had been purified to the point of complete self-possession could endure torture as bravely as Father Brébeuf did. His heart was conformed in such an impressive way to the Sacred Heart of Jesus that he could meet the maddening fury and hatred that brought his torture and death with prayers for his captors' souls.

Saint Jean de Brébeuf is a spectacular example of a man who used his passions to serve the greater good. Completely controlled by the help of God's grace, he was able to channel his enormous passion into a fervent love for the native peoples, especially the Huron nation. The fire and emotion in his heart and soul were put to the service of love and the Gospel. His self-possession gave him such strength during his torture and death that he was able to lay his life down in complete surrender, as an offering of love.

I am unaware of any martyr's death being gentle and painless, but Saint Jean's was especially brutal. For the sake of brevity, yet to honor this saint, here is a list of tortures that led to his death: He was stripped naked and forced to run a gauntlet, being beaten with sticks and clubs, then forced to walk in the cold. He had his fingers broken and his fingernails ripped off before his fingers were bitten off. He was hacked and stabbed. His bottom lip was cut off, and a hot iron was shoved down his throat. He had a ring of six hot hatchets placed around his neck, and hot water was poured over him to mock baptism. Strips of flesh from his legs and feet were cut off and eaten in front of him. His torturers cut off his nose, sliced off his upper lip, and hacked off a piece of his tongue. When he was already dead, they gauged out his eyes with a flaming stick, hacked off his feet, tore off his scalp, cut out his heart (to eat it), drank his blood, and finally split his jaw in two. Witnesses claimed his torture lasted four hours. All the while, his only utterances were prayers for Jesus to have mercy.

Saint Jean gives us an example to strive for. It was through the grace of God that Saint Jean was the man he was. This self-control is possible for all of us, and it is the goal we should hope, pray, and strive for. Saint Jean's story reveals what God can do in the life of any man if we let him. All we need to do are small acts of self-sacrifice (giving up salt, for example), and God can take us to incredible heights — even to that of heroic martyrdom.

•••

Each time we choose to put our passions in their proper place, leading us to act virtuously, we move one step closer to this self-possession. That, in turn, allows us to live much fuller lives. Our passions add such a spectacular dimension to our lives, often helping to move us in the direction of truth, beauty, and goodness.

To love is to give of ourselves fully without reservation or self-seeking. Pope Emeritus Benedict XVI wrote in his first encyclical, "Love is indeed 'ecstasy,' not in the sense of a moment of intoxication, but rather as a journey, an ongoing exodus out of the closed inward-looking self towards its liberation through self-giving, and thus towards authentic self-discovery and indeed the discovery of God."[23] Our passions can be great blessings in our attempts to give of ourselves. But when they draw us back into vice, quite the opposite occurs. If we keep giving in to impurities in our lives, we will lack the *ability* to love, because lust turns our love in on itself and makes us seek to fulfill only ourselves.

To love is to give of ourselves fully without reservation or self-seeking.

Barring sexual addictions,* we need to look at our sins of sexual impurity as they truly are: selfish and erroneous attempts to fulfill our own desires. Our struggles with anger can cloud our judgment so as to create an illusion that each of us is the only one on earth or one of only a few of any worth. Fear left unchecked can act like an anchor, preventing us from any noble action.

When we lack self-possession, we cannot give ourselves in true love, because no one can give what he doesn't have. If we don't possess our passions, we don't possess ourselves. We cannot then love in a selfless manner. We lack the freedom to lay down our lives and fulfill our duty to *shamar.*

When we don't govern them, our passions can be as damaging as an erupting volcano. How do we set about bringing them under control? There are a number of things we can do as we allow God's grace to penetrate our souls, purifying them bit by bit. Especially when it comes to get-

---

* If you are struggling with a pornography addiction, or any sexual addiction, it can be very difficult to get sober and fully recover. It is important to seek help in order to overcome the addiction and find freedom. I recommend three intense activities that will be the most effective in finding freedom: counseling with a certified sex-addiction therapist, spiritual direction, and a 12-step group such as Sexaholics Anonymous. Sometimes praying our way out of an addiction isn't possible — although God can always work miracles. The three activities above, coupled with daily prayer and frequenting the sacraments, will help you achieve the freedom you desire. The choice is yours.

ting lust under control, I suggest beginning with five steps outlined by John Robinson in *Spiritual Combat, Revisited*:

1. Avoid occasion of sin. If we struggle with pornography, occasion of sin might be surfing the internet or spending time on our smartphone when we are alone.
2. Fight sloth or laziness. Idleness can easily lead to daydreaming and fantasizing, which can then lead to sexual fantasizing and actions.
3. Develop the habit of obedience. This helps us channel our energies into serving others rather than constantly serving our own needs and desires.
4. Avoid making false judgments of others. Don't be easy on yourself and hard on others. Instead, be sure to judge your actions and sins in the clear light of truth.
5. Avoid thinking that you are more advanced then you are. In other words, don't think you have nailed the Christian life, especially when it comes to purity. Purity will be a struggle for most of your life. It's important for each of us to admit and accept this, so that we will not stray from the path in our pursuit of freedom.[24]

You might need counseling, a 12-step program, and a holy spiritual director to recover fully from your struggles. Whatever it is you need, seek it out and do everything you must do to be made free.

I also encourage you to ask Saint Jean de Brébeuf for help. This heroic preacher of the Gospel was a man in complete control of himself. One of the things that inspires me most about Saint Jean is the fact that, with God's grace and our cooperation, God can make us, like him, into men in complete possession of ourselves. If we go along for the ride, he can also do amazing things through us.

CHAPTER 4
Rise to Greatness

Whatever your task, work heartily,
as serving the Lord and not men.
Colossians 3:23

•••

Do few things, but do them well.
Saint Francis of Assisi

The University of San Diego, arguably one of the most beautiful college campuses in the country, sits on the hill next to Mission Bay. That is where I began my college days, with great hopes of becoming a football star and an academic powerhouse. Unfortunately, my football interests were quickly replaced with other activities that were easier and less tiring, such as drinking and being active in the social life. I soon found myself missing classes, getting the worst grades of my life, and adding girth to my midsection. By the year's end, I lost my academic scholarship and my buddies, and I had no place to live for the next school year. Since these were both fairly bad situations, I was shipped off to a far-distant place, the Midwest.

I ended up in Atchison, Kansas, at Benedictine College, a small Catholic school overlooking the Missouri River. In the middle of my junior year, my older brother talked my roommate and me into meeting with him for a Bible study once a week. My roommate and I were both quasi-Catholics, attending Mass (usually) on Sundays, but not embracing the Christian life. One night, after some discussion, my brother looked at both of us and told us we were potential leaders. He said that people were watching us, noticing us, but that we were wasting that gift of leadership because we weren't leading anyone anywhere positive. If anything, we were leading people in the wrong direction. If leadership is influence, ours was bad.

This taught me that everyone must ask himself, among other things, two questions:

What have I been given in life?

What am I doing with what I have been given?

Young men often perceive responsibility as a nasty thing. We like being boys old enough to do anything we want without the burden of duty weighing on our shoulders. We want to enjoy life, but we don't realize that this doesn't come from living for ourselves only. Every man is called to something beyond that. Every one of us is called to mature manhood, to leave our boyish ways behind. Sometimes that means facing fear, turning and accepting life as it comes to us, realizing that we are meant to serve others. Sometimes it means selling the PlayStation, turning off the TV, or putting the phone down to have a conversation with your wife about *her* day, to wrestle with your kids, or to be a friend to the roommate next to you.

Every one of us is called to mature manhood, to leave our boyish ways behind.

As Leonard Sax writes in *Boys Adrift*, "There's a long tradition of iconic American boys who disdain school, from Tom Sawyer to Ferris Bueller. But while those boys weren't heavily invested in school, they were still highly motivated to succeed — on their own terms, pursuing their own schemes."[25] He further explains, "The boys I am concerned about don't disdain school because they have other real-world activities they care about more. They disdain school because they disdain everything unless they can manipulate it on a screen. Nothing in the real world really excites them."[26] This is a problem. The apathy that is developing in young men is worrisome. These things may sound small, but it is often the small things that reveal who we are.

As we look at our lives and the world around us, do we swing for the fences or thrust our heads in the sand? Every one of us is called to be great. Yet how often do we settle, as if we are floating down a slow-flowing river, instead of constantly seeking to be excellent in the mission Our Lord has given us? Several years ago, I lived in New Jersey, serving as a missionary on a college campus. I occasionally played shuffleboard at a local bar, where there was a huge poster on the wall. The poster carried an anonymous quote: *I would rather die of thirst than drink from the cup of mediocrity.* If we really want to be the men God calls us to be, each of us should choose to live by this standard.

The Saint of Auschwitz

It was a serene October morning in 1982. Thousands of pilgrims were gathered in St. Peter's Square for the canonization of a Franciscan friar named Father Maximilian Kolbe. This Polish friar was a man for others, one who lived every moment in extraordinary ways.

As a boy, Maximilian (whose baptismal name was Raymond) once did something that displeased his mother. She asked him, "What will become of you?" When he heard this, instead of returning the question with a sarcastic remark, he sat for hours in front of an image of Our Lady and asked her with concern what *would* become of him. He recounted that Mary appeared to him holding two crowns in her hands, one red and the other white. "She looked on me with affection and asked me if I wanted those two crowns. The white one meant that I would remain pure, and the red, that I would be a martyr. I told her I accepted them. Then the Madonna looked at me sweetly and disappeared."[27]

When he was sixteen, Raymond entered the Franciscans and took the name Maximilian. He excelled at his seminary studies, and at the age of twenty-one, he earned his doctorate in philosophy at the Pontifical Gregorian University in Rome. He constantly stood out as a man of virtue and obedience, faithful in his devotion to Our Lady and his commitment to a life of virtue. His heart longed for the missions,[28] and his love for souls and Our Lady prompted him to start the *Militia Immaculatae*, or Knights of the Immaculata, with a few other brothers. Their purpose was to help souls in sin, schism, or heresy through the intercession of Mary Immaculate.

For a time, Father Kolbe joined some Franciscan companions on missions to China and Japan in order to set up the Knights of the Immaculata in the Far East. While there, they lived in extreme poverty so they could better fund their mission and print their publication, *The Knight*, in the native languages. They labored extensively to see this publication reach as many hands as possible to help draw people closer to Our Lord through Mary Immaculate. Father Kolbe dreamed of taking his Knights of the Immaculata to other areas of the world where Christianity was abandoned or hardly in existence, but he was elected superior of the friary he had founded in Poland, so, in obedience, he returned home.

In 1939, the Nazis invaded Poland. Father Kolbe had been preparing his brothers for this moment weeks before the first air raid hit the friary on September 7. Soon the Nazis realized that Kolbe was a man of influence. They began to search for information on him in hopes of declaring him treacherous. They couldn't find anything, so they made something up. Kolbe knew that the day of his imprisonment was approaching, and he began to prepare his brothers in the friary for persecution. On the morning of his arrest, the brothers remember seeing him in his good habit, the one reserved for Sunday and holy days. He knew that day would begin his journey to death.

As the Gestapo pulled up to arrest Father Kolbe, he walked outside to greet them with the words "Praised be Jesus Christ." He and four other priests were arrested; only two of the five would survive. They were taken to Pawiak Prison in Warsaw, a type of holding pen. There, Father Kolbe began his great work of consolation and aiding others in living through their sufferings with hope.

In May (the month of Mary) 1941, Maximilian arrived in Auschwitz, the camp that stood at the center of Nazi-occupied Europe. Even here, Father Kolbe would exhort his friends to pray for the Nazis, realizing that "no one's conversion is impossible."[29] The prisoners at Auschwitz were comforted to hear of Father Kolbe's arrival. As one person recollected, "We were glad to have such a real man, a fighter — a fighter for truth — with us."[30]

A fighter Maximilian proved himself to be, even in hell on earth. In an environment where death lingers in the shadows, animal instincts quickly take over as the main thrust in a person's thought processes. Living in constant fear and extreme hunger makes it easy to hope that the guy next to you dies, instead of you. Self-absorption becomes the norm, not sacrifice. Such was not the case for Father Kolbe. Love was his motive. He saw the great despair that pervaded the camp, the great suffering that all were forced to endure, and he chose to take as much of that suffering upon himself as possible, uniting it always to the Passion of Christ.

His sufferings were immense. He had pneumonia twice,

underwent an almost fatal beating by guards, and endured two of the hardest work assignments at the camp. Yet he still gave his bread rations to other prisoners. When other priests were afraid to preach during Masses said in secret, Father Kolbe stood and proclaimed the message of Christ. He brought hope to all around him, including several prisoners who had contemplated throwing themselves on the 220-volt wire fence surrounding the camp. Father Kolbe was a brilliant light shining in the darkest place on earth. One prisoner, in trying to describe the atrocity of Auschwitz, said it would take the pen of a Dante, the mind of a genius, to describe such a hell. Even in such a place as this, God was there in a powerful way through his humble fighter, Maximilian Kolbe.

In July 1941, the sirens of the camp began to wail. A prisoner had escaped from Block 14, the block Father Kolbe was in. The next morning, after the previous evening's search came up empty, the commander called the remaining prisoners out into the courtyard and announced that ten of them would die by starvation. He then selected ten men at random. One of them, named Gajowniczek, cried out, "My wife and my children!" The guards didn't care. He cried out again and again but was ignored. Suddenly there was movement in the ranks as someone pushed his way forward. The guards raised their rifles, ready to attack. It was Maximilian Kolbe, his step firm, his eyes confident and peaceful. They ordered him to stop, but he replied, "I want to talk to the commander." Oddly enough, he was neither shot nor beaten but was allowed to continue. "I want to die in place of this prisoner," Father Kolbe declared.[31] The men of Block 14 witnessed a saint give his life for a stranger. They witnessed the type of love Jesus Christ asks all of us to have.

The ten prisoners were led into the Penal Block. Once locked in, Father Kolbe was able to console those with him, helping them avoid a psychological breakdown that usually led prisoners to death within a few days. Not long after, he had them praying aloud, singing hymns, and reciting the Rosary. In their cell, with nothing but the floor to sit on and a bucket for urine, Father Maximilian Kolbe prepared his fellow prisoners for death. He helped them understand that God had not abandoned them, he heard their confessions, and he loved them as our heavenly Father loved them. Father Kolbe was a gift from God to those around him. He finally died by lethal injection on the evening of August 14, 1941, the vigil of the feast of the Assumption of Mary into heaven.

• • •

Maximilian Kolbe possessed great love and willingness to sacrifice. It can seem so hard for us to be able to rise to such a level of greatness. How did he accomplish it? He did it step by step. He was being prepared for heroism every day of his life, as he performed small acts of virtue. His entire life prepared him for his ultimate act of self-giving in the death camp. He was truly free to give his life then, because he had been free to give of himself in smaller ways thousands of times before.

For each one of us, this should be a huge inspiration. It's true for us, no matter what kind of greatness we aspire to. After all, Michael Jordan didn't come out of his mother's womb as the greatest player in NBA history (sorry, Lebron fans). He first had to crawl, then walk, then run, then dribble, then shoot, then finally become an all-star on the court. Troy Polamalu, the former safety of the Pittsburgh Steelers, did not go straight to the locker room after practice with his teammates. He stayed behind to do more drills. He didn't settle for where he was; he constantly pushed himself to something better. Mike Sweeney, a member of the Kansas City Royals Hall of Fame, was once told before spring training that he had a 0 percent chance of making the squad. He played the best spring ball of his life and eventually made five all-star appearances as the team captain. He did not tuck tail and run that day before spring ball.

Most of us aren't professional athletes. Nonetheless, we can learn something from the way athletes prepare themselves to achieve great things. They know that practice develops game-time habits. In our pursuit of greatness, this means practicing virtue and self-denial. In our society, where we have more comforts than anyone needs (from heated seats in our cars to smartphones and giant-screen TVs), we have so many means of satiating desires that we forget what it means to be great. Most of us are practicing for indulgence, not greatness. We forget that pushing ourselves even after it hurts can be great. We forget that giving up a small comfort can be great. We forget that sacrificing a desire in the moment for the sake of a greater good can be great. We need to be great in *all* the little moments so that when a big moment comes, we won't miss it. Our big moment may or may not mirror Saint Maximilian's, in the pit of a Nazi hell. That isn't the point. Hopefully we can strive to live lives that mirror his, because they allow for the freedom to be great. When we are blind to the invitations to this greatness, we

> *We need to be great in all the little moments so that when a big moment comes, we won't miss it.*

are not free to live our call as men, our call to *shamar*. But if we remain faithful in doing the small things well, it will have an impact on us. It will prepare us for the great things when they are asked of us. Every little good thing we do today will give us more freedom to do more good tomorrow with greater ease and joy. In this way, we prepare ourselves, with God's grace, step by step, to become men of greatness, in the image of Christ the King.

In your pursuit of true greatness, it might be helpful to cultivate a few habits:

- Determine a fast or mortification that directly targets areas where you are most easily tempted to seek comfort or give in to sloth. Be especially mindful of Wednesdays and Fridays, as these are days on which the Church asks us to make acts of penance.
- Focus on fewer things rather than on more, and strive to do them with excellence.
- Have someone in your life who can keep you accountable for your pursuit of greatness, especially related to your growth and goals.
- Set a reasonable standard for yourself in terms of what you think excellence should look like in your life. Be consistent in seeking to achieve that standard. Then, over time, as you grow, slowly and prudently raise that standard so as not to become stagnant.

CHAPTER 5
Combat Arrogance

He leads the humble in what is right,
and teaches the humble his way.
Psalm 25:9

• • •

Humility is the foundation of all the other virtues.
Saint Augustine

I have tried my hand a few times at elk hunting. Since I live in Colorado, which is said to have the highest elk population in the United States, I can't imagine not giving it a try. So far, though, I've had no luck. One of my friends once had the joy of making a kill — a kill of some sort, anyway. If you know anything about elk hunting, you know that it is not easy to find an elk, much less to get in a position to get a good shot. As his day of hunting was coming to a close, my buddy spotted a large animal, sighted it in, pulled the trigger, and saw it fall. No doubt the adrenaline kicked in. I can't wait for that experience. The one thing about my buddy's hunt I do not envy — the result. It turns out he accidentally got a moose instead.

I think this story helps illustrate the fact that often in life we fail to see reality clearly. Why does this matter? Because, if we want to follow Christ faithfully, we need to see ourselves (and the world around us) as we truly are. If we want to follow Christ faithfully, we need to see ourselves (and the world around us) as we truly are. If I can't see things in my life as they really are, I can't allow God's grace to transform me. I become blind to my need for Christ. This is why we have to be humble. Humility is often described as seeing ourselves as we truly are, which is why humility is said to be the foundational virtue. Without it, we fail to see our desperate dependence on God's grace and mercy.

If we are serious about pursuing freedom and becoming

the men we're meant to be, we need humility. Why? Because if we don't see ourselves clearly, we don't know what in our lives and actions needs to change. If I am humble, I will see

If we want to follow Christ faithfully, we need to see ourselves (and the world around us) as we truly are.

areas where I am weak in virtue and will seek out opportunities to grow. More importantly, I will ask the Lord for help. If I am not humble and don't see the areas where I am weak, I won't grow as I should, and I won't recognize my need for God's grace. Without humility, my

pursuit of freedom will be stalled because of my lack of clear sight. I will be aiming for an elk and end up staring at a dead moose.

The Father of the Greatest Saint of Modern Times
Louis Martin, the father of Saint Thérèse of Lisieux, was in tune with God from an early age. As a young man, he wanted to enter religious life. This is where his growth in humility began to take center stage. When he sought to enter a religious order, they turned him away because he had not studied Latin. He took it in stride and returned home to study. For more than a year, he hit the Latin books, hoping the religious order would give him a second chance. When an illness disrupted this plan, he decided it was God's providence leading him down a different path. So, with a heavy heart, he surrendered his hope for religious life.

Instead, he set up his own watchmaker's shop, to which he later added a jewelry shop. He became a businessman who had his eyes solely fixed on the Lord. At thirty-four, he married Zélie Guerin, a young woman who had also desired religious life. Instead, she had launched a lace-making enterprise. These two entrepreneurs first planned to live their marriage as brother and sister.[32] Slowly, they discovered that marriage was God's plan for them, and they humbly accepted this and were shortly after ready to accept the arrival of children into their marriage. Louis entered each day with a humble spirit, hoping to see clearly what God wanted for him. For example, he did not insist on becoming religious because it was a holier way of life than marriage; instead, he trusted that the Lord desired to make him holy in a different way, and he followed God's will.

As a further demonstration of Louis's tremendous humility, he eventually walked away from his own business to help his beloved wife thrive in hers. But his greatest show of humility would come at the end of his life, when he suffered a debilitating illness. In 1887, as he was nearing his sixty-fourth birthday, Louis developed cerebral arteriosclerosis, which caused temporary paralysis, strokes, and attacks on his mental faculties. Almost a year later, he began having hallucinations. Thankfully, his health improved temporarily, and God's goodness allowed him to walk his dear youngest daughter, Thérèse, to the altar for her investiture in the Carmelite Order.

His intense suffering and humiliation would increase months later. At one point, "he thought that the revolution was at the gates of the city, and he grabbed a gun to defend his Carmelite daughters. Céline and Léonie were the only ones who witnessed this atrocious scene and were not able to succeed in reasoning with him."[33] After that, Louis was confined to a mental asylum. Rumors began to circulate around the town. "People claimed that Louis's austerity led to his condition, or that he had syphilis, or that his daughters were responsible for his state because of the grief they caused in leaving him."[34] During his time in the asylum, he had moments of complete lucidity — enough for him to understand where he was and what was going on. One of the religious who worked in the asylum told Louis that he was an apostle for the sick people around him. Louis replied, "I would rather be an apostle elsewhere! However, since it is the Will of God! I believe it is to humble my pride."[35] Another time, Louis expressed to his doctor, "I know why God has sent me this trial. I never had any humiliation in my life; I needed one."[36]

During his three years in the asylum, he consistently prayed in the chapel and received the Eucharist whenever his condition allowed. He knew he must depend on the grace of God and be strengthened by him in his time of suffering and humiliation. Once he was no longer a threat to anyone (his legs suffered a permanent paralysis), he was finally released. Two days later, he was brought to see his daughters at Carmel. "He wasn't able to speak, but he seemed to understand what his daughters said to him. And when they said goodbye, he managed to point his index finger upward and articulate 'in heaven'."[37]

Louis Martin died two years later, on July 29, 1894, a Sunday morning. His daughter Céline was with him as he left this life. She wrote to her sisters in Carmel about the experience:

> Papa is in heaven. I received his last sigh, and closed his eyes. His fine countenance immediately took on an expression of happiness and profound peace. Serenity is marked on his features. He died quietly at a quarter past eight. My poor heart burst at the last moment, and a flood of tears bathed his bed. But

underneath I was really glad for his happiness after the terrible martyrdom which he has undergone
and which we have shared with him.[38]

Saint Louis Martin gives us a profound example of knowing
ourselves clearly and accepting the humiliations granted by
Our Lord to free us from the grasp of pride.

• • •

To allow the grace of God to make us who we were made to
be, we need to see ourselves as we are right now. We have to
know our starting place in order to plot the course to our
destination. Humility is the virtue that shows us our starting point and helps us to see the path and the steps we need
to take to reach our goal. We see what we need because of
our humility and thus can allow other virtues in our lives
to build.

Let's use athletics as an analogy. Athletes often study
film. They watch other players for inspiration, and they watch
themselves on film to critique their style and techniques.
They watch their opponents so they can find their weaknesses. In short, athletes (and coaches) watch lots of film so
they can see themselves as they truly are. We, as followers of
Christ, should be motivated by this. Though we don't neces-
sarily need a GoPro on our head all day long, we do need to
be conscious of who we are and what we do each day. A daily
review of our lives can be a big help in this. We can do an examination of our day by running through it in our heads as if
we were reviewing a video. We can reflect on the good things
we did and the dumb things we did. This habit also equips us
to see patterns that are developing in our lives.

Doing these daily examinations has allowed me to see when I was too hard on my kids, ate too much, didn't love my wife well, and so forth. I can see patterns and bring them to our Lord and ask for the particular graces I need. I can also seek help and put in place accountability, if necessary. But if I don't know my issues, I can't get the help I need. I will remain a man who isn't free to be who God wants me to be.

One way God shows his fatherly care is by allowing us moments of humiliation. For example, sometimes I'll get rolling at work for a few days or weeks, thinking I'm amazing. Then it hits. Something lays me flat for a few minutes or hours. Perhaps I make a fool of myself somehow, have a solid critique come my way, or just forget to do something I was supposed to do. Even though it can be difficult, I know that this is how Our Lord, in his mercy, keeps me humble. Thanks be to God. I know that if my arrogance grows, it will create a blindness that can be all-encompassing. God allows us all to experience these moments of humiliation to keep us on the path of humility. If we can accept these moments, reflect on them, and allow ourselves to be humbled by them, we will slowly be set free to live as we were created to live.

Humility helps us to see that we are totally dependent on the grace of God. This can be tough. Men often don't like to ask for directions or seek help for much of anything. When we refuse to seek help in our journey of discipleship, we end up in a bad place fast. Humility keeps us rooted in the simple truth that nothing good that we do comes from us — it is all a grace. Humility is the virtue working in our souls that prevents our eyes from being shut to this reality. You and I need the grace of God in our lives in order to become who he wants us to be. We need to see that each moment of every day. When we lose sight of this reality, we quickly become arrogant, and arrogance leads us down the path to hell.

If we want to live humility, we should also accept all that God has given us — our gifts, talents, accomplishments, and graces, as well as our shortcomings. Some of us, in our desire to be humble, go a bit too far. Often we reject or downplay our talents, gifts, and accomplishments, because we want to be humble. When someone compliments us, our response is to brush

Humility keeps us rooted in the simple truth that nothing good that we do comes from us — it is all a grace.

it off, give credit somewhere else, or reject it altogether. This is false humility. It's false, because it contradicts the truth of who we are and what we're capable of. If humility is to see ourselves as we truly are, then rejecting who we are isn't humility. Sometimes we do it from a desire to hear more flattery; other times it is a scrupulous self-criticism. Whatever the motive, it is not humility. The truly humble person simply responds with "thank you" to compliments if they are true and deserved.

As a husband and a father, Saint Louis reminds us that God wants all of us to mirror his Son, who was meek and humble of heart. Saint Louis knew his dependence on the Lord and his need for humiliations, and his soul was prepared to do the Lord's bidding. Pride is the greatest of sins, and humility counters it. Let's seek to be men living in the freedom of clarity. Let's strive to allow God to transform us into forces of nature, starting where we are. It's the only way forward.

As you pursue humility, here are some helpful daily exercises to bring into your life. I recommend that you commit to all of them.

- Make a daily examination of conscience.
- Accept humiliations mindfully when they come.
- Consistently recognize your complete dependence on God. You might perhaps say a simple prayer each day, or you could recite Psalm 25:9 from the start of this chapter.
- Strive to respond to compliments and gratitude with a simple "thank you," rather than exercising false humility by rejecting them.
- Allow others to speak truth into your life to help you see yourself more clearly. In particular, accept criticisms or corrections that come to you, if they are just and accurate.

CHAPTER 6

Become Unbreakable

Blessed is the man who endures trial, for when he has stood the test he will receive the crown of life which God has promised to those who love him.
James 1:12

• • •

Hear me well: I am quite certain that if you struggle, you will be a saint.
Saint Josemaría Escrivá

During my senior year in high school, I was the starting quarterback. The season was going very well, and we headed into the state finals ranked second in the state. We lost. To make it even worse, I didn't play particularly well. The next day, the all-state selections came out in the paper. I was second team all-state ... behind the quarterback of the team that beat us in the finals. I remember walking into my room that day and finding a note my brother had left there. It was a copy of Theodore Roosevelt's speech "Man in the Arena." It remains one of my favorite inspiring compositions. So much so that I think it is worth quoting in its entirety:

> It is not the critic who counts; not the man who points out how the strong man stumbles, or where the doer of deeds could have done them better. The credit belongs to the man who is actually in the arena, whose face is marred by dust and sweat and blood; who strives valiantly; who errs, who comes short again and again, because there is no effort without error and shortcoming; but who does actually strive to do the deeds; who knows great enthusiasms, the great devotions; who spends himself in a worthy cause; who at the best knows in the end the triumph of high achievement, and who at the worst, if he fails, at least fails while daring greatly, so that

his place shall never be with those cold and timid
souls who neither know victory nor defeat.

Note how Roosevelt stresses the importance of effort. The
man willing to compete is the one to be praised, not the crit-
ic who never even tries. In every pursuit in our lives, we likely will face ups and downs. Many things won't be easy. In
numerous instances, we will fail. Yet we need to be resilient,
especially as we seek to answer the call to guard and protect.

Playing competitive sports taught me that when you hit
the ground, you either get up or get trampled. Lying around
and taking in the view isn't an option for an athlete. Athletes
quickly realize that hitting the ground happens often, and
it is part of sports. I am thankful for my experience as an
athlete, because it prepared me for the reality that life hits
hard as well; it can be tempting to stay on the ground and
watch life go by, but this is not the way to respond. Instead,
we need to be resilient in the face of setbacks and failures.
In today's culture of comfort, perhaps no one understands
this as well as athletes. I remember seeing on the sideline
at a rugby tournament a guy with a hole through part of
his mouth. Nonetheless, he was drinking whiskey. He didn't
stay on the ground where that cleat went through his face.
He jumped up and got back into the game.

I, for one, appreciate modern comforts. I am grateful for
air conditioning and clean water piped into my home. I am
not grateful for how easy it is to roll over and give up when
life gets hard. But men who are living their call to *shamar* do
not simply roll over when things get tough. Here's an example. When Joe Rantz was fifteen years old, his father drove
away with his stepmother and stepbrothers in their station
wagon. He told Joe he needed to stay there to make it on his

own. Alone, without much food left in the house, Joe woke the next morning, wiped the tears from his eyes, and made himself a cup of coffee. He made the decision to survive, not to give up. Joe's life was riddled with difficulties. Yet he didn't quit. He found his way to college, the rowing team, and won a gold medal in the 1936 Olympics — right under the nose of Hitler. I would have to guess that most young men today wouldn't make it as well as Joe did back then — at least it sure seems that way.

If we want to live out our call to *shamar*, we must learn resiliency. Without it, guarding and protecting our families and the culture becomes impossible. We need to be willing and able to suffer well for the sake of our souls and the souls of others. We need to be able to pick up our crosses and follow Christ. Remember, Christ

We need to be willing and able to suffer well for the sake of our souls and the souls of others.

fell three times while carrying his cross to redeem the world, but he was resilient. He got back up each time and kept going.

How often have we failed in our duty to make this world a better place and promote the Gospel because we weren't willing to get back up? Because we were too soft to endure the hard knocks and difficulties?

How often have we made excuses?

The Priest Who Suffered with the Lepers

Jozef ("Jef") De Veuster was born on January 3, 1840, in Belgium. He joined the Sacred Heart Fathers in 1858 and took the name Damien. In 1863, he responded to the call for missionaries in Hawaii. He was ordained a priest in 1864 and was sent to the district of Puna. At this time, Hawaii was missionary territory, and about one-third of the native population was Catholic. Damien had the care of about 350 souls. Not long after his arrival, leprosy began to spread in Hawaii. In 1865, a decree from the government called for segregation of leprosy victims, and Molokai was chosen as a leprosarium. The Church sent a priest to minister to them once a year and had a chapel, dedicated to Saint Philomena, built for those who had been banished. They desired to have a more frequent priestly presence, knowing that death could come knocking well within a year's time, between the priest's visits. The local bishop asked his priests for volunteers, unwilling to assign anyone to this difficult task. Father Damien immediately jumped to his feet and offered himself for the sake of the lepers. He was to become the first resident pastor of Molokai, a post he would never leave.

It wasn't long after Father Damien's arrival among the lepers that his need to be resilient manifested itself. Not having a fondness for Catholics, the board of health in Honolulu protested against Damien and his work in Molokai. They gave him permission to minister there, with the catch that he could never leave the infected community. This meant he could not minister to the other local communities or visit fellow priests so they could hear his confessions. Damien didn't flinch and faithfully remained pastor to the forgotten. In one instance, a brother priest came to hear his confession. The captain of his vessel would not allow the priest off the ship, nor would he take Father Damien on board. Knowing the crew didn't speak French, Father Damien shouted his confession in French to his fellow priest, who shouted back absolution as the ship pulled away. Such was the tenacity of Father Damien. This character trait would be imperative throughout the rest of his life.

The lepers themselves proved difficult, as despair had permeated their minds and hearts. Father Damien watched "the degradation and the consequences of life reduced to the levels of brute survival and animal pleasures. He understood what had prompted the revolting orgies and debaucheries that were taking place ... but he did not intend that they should continue."[39] Father Damien took care of his flock as a mother would care for her young. He tried to visit each person once a week, bandaging each leper's wounds, cleaning them, cutting away rotten flesh, sweeping floors, and the like. One biographer relates: "This was not done with grace and calm from the start. Damien admitted freely that in the first weeks he had to leave the sides of the patients again and again, staggering outside to retch and lose the contents of his stomach. At other times, he suffered blinding headaches because of the stench coupled with the nervous tension that developed as a result of his close contact with the lepers in his act of ministering to them."[40]

As hard as the work was, Father Damien enjoyed peace and pastoral joy in the early years. Later, he had to endure evil rumors that he was leading a life of immorality. Because he was alone on the island, and because many at the time believed leprosy was a sexually transmitted disease, some assumed that he "was living an immoral life on Molokai, mingling freely with the native women in their debaucheries."[41] In 1884, Father Damien finally came down with leprosy himself. He hoped to make it to Honolulu the next year to try a new treatment, but his superiors denied him, "accusing him of being egotistical and certainly devoid of all tact and delicacy."[42] Father Damien experienced much slander in his lifetime and even after he died. His work was not easy, and the persecutions he faced, among his own superiors and beyond, must have been exhausting and demoralizing. But Father Damien was a man of resilience. He remained strong as he served a forgotten people in a faraway land. He truly was the "hero of Molokai."

Father Damien, with so many attacks coming at him, neared the end of his life knowing exactly the suffering that was to come. He had watched hundreds of people die of leprosy. He consoled himself at night by walking through the cemetery, praying the Rosary and thinking of each person he buried there. Though he knew what his death would be like, he had no way of knowing how he would be remembered — and he did not care. All he was concerned about was intimacy with God and the souls of his flock. He died on April 15, 1889.

• • •

God desires to use each of us to rock the gates of hell. He desires to use our every difficulty to make us great, to sanctify us. He wants us to be men unwilling to relent even under the weight of the cross. When we become resilient, we have the capacity, with God's grace, to become saints like Father Damien.

When my five-year-old son says he can't do something, my immediate response is, "You need to try." I love watching him then make an effort and succeed. It expands his vision of what is possible and teaches him that, often, extended effort can be met with successful results. I don't want him to develop a sense of limits that are simply untrue or the tendency to make excuses when he faces something difficult. Last year, he asked me (of his own volition) to take the training wheels off his bike. Later that day, he was riding in the backyard on his own, no training wheels in sight. It's incredible to watch his mental transformation every time he learns that he can do difficult things. And this is possible for all of us. It starts with refusing to make excuses in the face of life's tough demands.

Making excuses is easy. We allow our excuses to impede our pursuit of greatness and to poison our mental pictures of ourselves. Excuses shape our lives according to our impairments, and this makes us less free to grow and to follow our call. Excuses seem to give us freedom; after all, we use them to free ourselves from expectations and responsibility. Although we might feel free, we are, in fact, falling further into slavery to our weaknesses and perceived limitations. We lessen our ability to live in true freedom. Our reality becomes blurred, and our actions become more frivolous. We become self-centered and weak. Excuses are a virus.

Resilience gives us the strength to refuse to let suffering, hardship, and challenges keep us from pursuing what we are called to pursue.

When Jesus Christ told us that the gates of hell would not withstand the kingdom of God, he meant it. He is calling us to a pursuit of truth and love that will rattle the very gates of hell. Resilience gives us the strength to refuse to let suffering, hardship, and challenges keep us from pursuing what we are called to pursue. When we live like this, the Devil fears what God is capable of doing through us. Resilient men, faithful to Jesus Christ, will build the kingdom of God and blast open the gates of hell.

Remember that another remarkable aspect of being a

resilient disciple of Christ is that it changes us. God is constantly showering his grace upon us. This grace builds upon the natural capacity growing in our souls as we face the struggles of living lives of integrity. As we push to be resilient, God's grace sharpens us. He sanctifies us. When we seek to keep Christ at the center of our lives, everything we do will change us, if we recognize it and allow it.

We sharpen knives against stone. During the sharpening process, the knife loses a portion of itself to be made sharp once again. And so it is for us. When we bounce back, as men of faith, we can trust that we never bounce back as the same men. We are slowly transformed by the hardship and made more into the saints God desires us to be. In the words of Saint Alphonsus Liguori, "If during life we have embraced everything as coming from God's hands, and if at death we embrace death in fulfillment of God's holy will, we shall certainly save our souls and die the death of saints. Let us then abandon everything to God's good pleasure, because being infinitely wise, he knows what is best for us; and being all-good and all-loving — having given his life for us — he wills what is best for us."[43]

God allows us to suffer, because he knows it will change us. It is up to each of us to decide whether we will let our sufferings change us for the better. Like Father Damien of Molokai, let's ask God for the grace to let our sufferings and setbacks strengthen us and draw us closer to him, setting us free to pursue him with greater love and determination.

As you pursue resilience, here are some questions to ponder:

- When and why do I typically make excuses?

- What types of hardship, suffering, or challenge do I let become burdensome or overwhelming to me?
- Where am I refusing to get back up and be resilient?
- How do I typically justify the ease with which I quit?

CHAPTER 7
Surrender Control

For whoever would save his life will lose it; and whoever loses his life for my sake and the gospel's will save it.

Mark 8:35

• • •

God gives each one of us sufficient grace ever to know His holy will, and to do it fully.

Saint Ignatius of Loyola

I recently saw a picture of Jack Flaherty hugging his mom after one of his games. Jack had just helped his team, the St. Louis Cardinals, to a victory from the mound against the Atlanta Braves in Game 5 of the playoffs. The picture with his mom was sweet and touching, but a few pieces of background make it even more inspiring. Jack was adopted by his mom, a single mother, when he was three weeks old. She ended up adopting another boy, and Jack was an older brother. But one particular day in Jack's life stood out to me as I read about him. He was a freshman in high school and headed over to his younger brother's game. He told his mom all the reasons he was done with baseball. She patiently listened and affirmed him that it was his choice. She then laid out two conditions necessary if he was to quit: (1) He had to call the coach and tell him. (2) He had to walk over to his brother's team, explain to those younger boys why he was going to quit, and tell them that it is okay to quit when the going gets rough. Jack went to practice the next day. What a mom!

As we reflected on resilience in a previous chapter, hopefully this story resonates with that concept of not folding when something gets tough. Jack was challenged to be resilient, and he responded. We can fall on either side of the spectrum — quit too easily or be so stubborn that we never relent. Both tendencies come from our desire to be self-reliant. While we need to take responsibility for our lives and actions, the desire to rely solely on our own strength and abilities can destroy us. We're not meant to live that way.

As much as we hate to admit it, there are times when surrender is necessary. By "surrender" I don't mean quitting; I mean letting go of control. This can be one of the hardest things a man has to do.

As men, in our call to lead, guard, and protect, we often seek to control every facet of every situation. We want to call the shots, give the orders, do it our way. This goes beyond simply not asking for help. Too often, we want to make everything in life go our way — just think of the classic Frank Sinatra song "My Way." As men and as Christians, our goal in life should never be to do things our way. That simply isn't how the God of all creation designed things to be, and the attempt to live this way leads to destruction, desperation, loneliness, and frustration. Our goal in life should be to do things God's way. Though our duty to guard and protect sometimes means that we need to make decisions, we are meant to do so as servants and in obedience to God's will.

The desire to be masters of our own universe can seep into our relationships, our work, and everyday occurrences, no matter how small. It can lead to rebellion in our children, suppression among our colleagues, and unhappiness in our spouses. In short, it can be very damaging. This means that our temptation to control can severely hinder our ability to guard and protect. It suffocates our freedom by boxing us into our prison of self-sufficiency. As we reflected in an earlier chapter on humility, all good comes from God. Our need for him is real and fundamental. Can we surrender our urge to be "self-made" enough to let him lead us? Humility and surrender are closely linked.

My work among college athletes often brings the struggle of self-sufficiency to the surface. These young men are tremendously talented and successful in athletics. They have put countless hours into securing their continued achievement, in the weight room, in studying film, in practice, and so forth. Unfortunately, they easily begin to think that, just as in athletics, everything in their lives depends on their hard work. Many of us can relate to this in some area of our lives. We pull the reins close to our chest. We begin to assume too much credit. Slowly, we become our own "gods," though we don't usually realize it. Then, when situations occur that don't seem to line up with the direction we thought we were headed in, when plans don't fall into place as we expected them to, frustration sets in. Over time, this can even turn into bitterness. We keep trying to control the pieces of our lives even though we can never know what life will bring. Anxiety and stress build up until we are like volcanoes waiting to erupt. Self-sufficiency sounds cool, but it becomes a prison — one that enslaves men everywhere.

The ability to surrender, or simply to let go, allows us to be men who follow where the Lord leads.

Surrendering to God doesn't mean we passively sit back since he's going to do what he wants. God is in charge, but we still need to be active. We are part of this journey as his sons. He wants us to participate. The ability to surrender, or simply to let go, allows us to be men who follow where the Lord leads. Recognizing that we aren't in control of our lives brings peace and joy, but to get to that point, we have to move. It is analogous to walking through an unknown space blindfolded while someone else leads us. If we don't step, we won't get anywhere. If we don't let ourselves be led, we will not make any progress.

Guardian of the Holy Family

The man who became the earthly father of Jesus Christ set the precedent for us in surrendering to the will of God. Even though Saint Joseph does not speak a single word in Scripture, he is still *the* man.

Often, my friends and I will joke about how we "married up." Well, Saint Joseph is the ultimate guy who "married up"; his bride was the Blessed Virgin Mary, a woman completely free from sin. Joseph possessed immense holiness, and his union with God was profound. He wrestled with many painful circumstances, beginning with the discovery that Mary was pregnant before they lived together — and he was not the father. He considered divorcing her. The Gospel of Matthew describes how God intervened in the situation: "As he considered this, behold, an angel of the Lord appeared to him in a dream, saying, 'Joseph, son of David, do not fear to take Mary your wife, for that which is conceived in her is of the Holy Spirit; she will bear a son, and you shall call his name Jesus, for he will save his people from their sins" (Mt 1:20–21). Joseph accepted the mystery of his new spouse and the Son she carried. He was called to be the father of this child, even to name the child, and to protect his spouse. As a faithful Jew, no doubt Joseph understood the significance of raising the Messiah, but he had no idea how it would play out in real life. His surrender displays an exceptional amount of trust. As Pope Saint John Paul II said of him, "What he did is the clearest 'obedience of faith.'"[44]

The birth of Jesus was another immense moment of surrender. Here is Saint Joseph, arriving with Mary in Bethlehem with the birth of the Messiah imminent. When they get there, he can't get a room. Nothing. Just a manger among the animals and their stench. The guardian of the Redeemer didn't lose his cool when he recognized that the Savior of the world was to be born in this setting — at least, nothing in Scripture speaks of this. He no doubt surrendered this moment to the will of God. He trusted his heavenly Father and sought to serve Mary in any way possible.

Then, shortly after the birth of his Son, he had another dream — the kind all of us want to have, in which God's voice is clearly heard and communicated (even if via an angel). "Now when they had departed, behold, an angel of the Lord appeared to Joseph in a dream and said, 'Rise, take the child and his mother, and flee to Egypt, and remain there till I tell you; for Herod is about to search for the child, to destroy him.' And he rose and took the child and his mother by night, and departed to Egypt" (Mt 2:13–14). Here we see Joseph's virtue shine again. He trusted what he heard and took his family to safety. He did not doubt the message or ignore it, thinking he could protect his family and telling himself, "It probably isn't that bad." His response to the Lord's will was immediate. He did not seek to control the situation by waiting around to ask his neighbors in Bethlehem if anyone had seen soldiers or heard of any trouble brewing in the distance. He simply did what God asked of him. No questions asked.

Another scene in Scripture reminds us of the surrender in which Saint Joseph lived his life. The Gospel of Luke recounts how Mary and Joseph lost twelve-year-old Jesus for three days. The Holy Family had made their pilgrimage to Jerusalem for the Passover. On their journey home, Mary and Joseph realized that Jesus was not with them or their acquaintances. Finally, after three days, they found him in the Temple. Mary asked her young Son, "Why have you treated us so? Behold, your father and I have been looking for you anxiously." Jesus replied: "How is it that you sought me? Did you not know that I must be in my Father's house?" (Lk 2:48–49). When you juxtapose Mary's words, "your father and I," with Jesus', "my Father's house," you get a sense of the mystery in which Joseph lived his life. He was called to guard the Redeemer and his immaculate mother while seeking to engage fully in life with its many unknowns and unanswered questions. Yet he continued to surrender and offer his life as a sacrifice to the activity of redeeming the world that his Son came to accomplish.

Although we have no recorded words of Saint Joseph, we know he was a man of action. He heard the word of God and acted. He remains a model, even with the little we know of him, for every one of us men. He trusted the Lord deeply, never hesitated to do his will, and offered his life at the service of the salvation of souls. He stands for each of us as a model of laying down control of our lives and letting God lead. His life testifies to what it means to surrender all things for the greater glory of God. May we seek his help in doing the same.

• • •

When we seek to control our lives, we put all the pressure on ourselves. We think it is up to us to accomplish our goals, find our paths, fix mistakes (our own or those of others), and to do it all on the exact timeline we have set in our minds. We act as if life is a storybook that we are able to craft along the way. Though it might be scratch-and-sniff, it sure isn't choose-your-own-adventure. Life has too many unknowns, too many surprises, too many variables. Thinking we can control our own destinies is not only impossible; it is also foolish. Yet, time and time again, we slip into thinking this way. We get impatient at slow results or frustrated with a nuanced outcome that touched on our hopes but failed to give us everything we wanted.

I imagine all of us can recall a moment or two in our lives when we tried to maintain control: picking our colleges or majors, finding our spouses, settling into our careers, hitting our financial goals, determining our family size or the perfect city to live in. I remember when I was single and hoping to find the love of my life. I was impatient with God's timing and became a bit of a brute with both God and some of the women I dated along the way to finding my amazing wife. I wanted things my way and now. Yet the Lord, in his timing, had different plans. I didn't surrender well to them, and this caused tension in my life that I could have avoided had I simply let go. What I failed to remember was that God knows us, that he loves us, and that he wants what is best for us.

Many of us also seek to control the smaller things that come up each day. Our daily routine can be a big area of control. I know that my weekend plans to chop firewood or clean the garage might not be the activities my wife or children need from me that day. Am I willing to let go and seek the Lord's will in that moment? Am I willing to be a dad and a husband and serve the needs of my family? Do my friends need my time or help in some way? It's not just the big things we need to surrender to God; we also need to surrender in these small moments when he asks us to serve him, to do his will, to live for others.

What is our outlook then? If we can't take the reins but must be active, what does that look like? Saint Ignatius knew these tendencies to control and the questions that arise when we are faced with the need to surrender. In his *Spiritual Exercises*, he guides us to develop what he calls "holy indifference."[45] This is a spectacular way to describe the challenge to surrender. Holy indifference doesn't mean we are apathetic about everything. It simply means that we care only about what God wants. Our indifference is to the outcome, but we simultaneously have a strong desire to see God's will fulfilled.

Living holy indifference isn't easy. If we seek to serve the Lord as men trying to guard the proclamation of truth in love, we will have thorns in our sides. Living a life of discipleship is not easy. Our Lord himself died on a cross before he rose from the dead. We, too, are asked to carry our crosses. Often we will find ourselves in situations in which we would rather remove the thorns or drop the cross in hopes of proceeding according to our own plans. Or we just might

The task at hand is to look upward and ask the Lord what he desires for us ... and then to surrender to his desire.

want something a lot, yet that isn't what the Lord wills for us in that moment. These are also tough situations that require surrender, and the more we develop holy indifference, the better equipped we will be to face these moments. The task at hand is to look upward and ask the Lord what he desires for us ... and then to surrender to his desire.

He is our Father and desires what is best for us. Often, we will not be privy to his plans until they happen. This is hard for many of us, because we want to see the future, but we can't. Instead, the best path forward — and the one that allows us the most joy in life — is to trust God. "For I know the plans I have for you, says the LORD, plans for welfare and not for evil, to give you a future and a hope" (Jer 29:11). Thankfully, we have Saint Joseph in our corner. He is not only a tremendous example for us; he is also a powerful helper when we ask him for his intercession.

When we respond to God's grace and surrender to him, we allow our joy to grow. Anxiety and bitterness begin to dissipate. In fact, this is cause for great peace, because our lives are not our own, so we can stop trying to control them. When we recognize this and begin to live accordingly, our ears can hear the voice of the Lord more effectively. We are able to respond to our call to *shamar*, since we will hear, see, and respond to the Lord as servants eager to serve. We fight *his* battles, rather than those battles we create for ourselves by our feeble attempts to be self-made.

As I have said, we have a tendency to seek to control. Pursuing surrender is hard but transformative. Here are some helpful things to keep in mind as you work to let go of control:

- Surrender doesn't mean letting life go on cruise control.
- Asking God to show you his will can be challenging, and it's a good idea to seek wise counsel, perhaps in spiritual direction, to help you hear his voice.
- Find moments throughout the day to intentionally let go of your preference in favor of someone else's preference.
- Try to recognize when you are insisting on things. Then take time to pray and reflect on those moments. Are you taking it to the point of seeking control?

- Are there certain things the Church teaches that you overlook or ignore simply because they don't suit you? When we do this,
  we might be exerting a type of damaging
  control over our lives, and it is wise to pray
  for the grace to surrender to the authority
  of the Church.

CHAPTER 8
Embrace the Mission

Go therefore and make disciples of all nations.
Matthew 28:19

• • •

We have been called to heal wounds, to unite what has fallen apart, and to bring home those who have lost their way.
Saint Francis of Assisi

I was in my first year as a Catholic missionary with the Fellowship of Catholic University Students (FOCUS). My job was to share the Gospel with college students, lead them in small-group Bible studies, and mentor them so that they could become evangelists as well. I was fairly fresh in my own decision to follow Jesus as a disciple. Because of that, I was still not completely comfortable saying the name of Jesus out loud. We didn't do that a lot as Catholics, at least not in my experience. When I did, I would feel myself blush and then have to repress my vanity so I could keep talking. As a missionary, my job (and my hope) was to help the young men in front of me come to know Jesus Christ and give their lives to him, to make him the center of their lives. If I was going to do this, I really needed to get over my lack of comfort in saying the name of Jesus — and fast. I know I am not the only Christian man who is or has been hesitant to talk about Jesus and his faith. I get it. Yet it is part of our duty. When I recognized that, I pushed through. I had to do it. The beautiful thing is, the more we say the name of Jesus, the easier it becomes. I think I can confidently say now that I love opportunities to mention Jesus.

A clear mission that comes to us as disciples of Christ is that of making him known. It's a mission that can be intimidating. It is also a proactive aspect of protection — to help shape and form the souls of those around us.

We enjoy talking about things that we love. Most of us

will boldly hype up the new burger joint if we enjoy the food there. We love our favorite teams, and most of us proudly wear their jerseys around town (sometimes even to Mass). And if we really love Jesus, we will want to talk about him all the time. If we are going to see a change in the culture around us, we must speak of Jesus Christ. We need to invite those around us to put him at the center of their lives, to have an intimate friendship with him. As Pope Saint Paul VI wrote, the Church exists to evangelize.[46] This becomes our mission the moment we are baptized. As Christians, we are hardwired to talk about Jesus.

What is the message we are called to proclaim? It is the most basic truth in history: Jesus Christ died for our sins. Sin had created a chasm between us and God, and we were no longer able to have intimacy with God as we did in the Garden of Eden. No matter what efforts we put forth (as highlighted throughout the Old Testament), we were never able to reach across that chasm. So God, in his perfect love for us, became one of us so that he, in the person of Jesus Christ, could reach across that gap and create the possibility of friendship once again. He invites us to live this friendship in his Church, where he gives himself to us through the sacraments.

Spreading the truth of the Gospel doesn't mean just telling everyone that abortion is bad, sex before marriage is bad, missing Sunday Mass is bad, etc., etc. The Gospel message is the relationship behind the "rules." Truth is love incarnate. Jesus is the fulfillment of love and truth, and proclaiming truth is proclaiming Jesus. The early apostles knew this deeply. They traveled the world to proclaim the story of Jesus Christ, a story no one knew. The people they spoke to had no Christian background at all. The apostles had to look people in the eye and talk about a man who was God and died on a cross at the hands of the Roman government but then came to life again. And the apostles were all, apart from Saint John, killed for telling this story.

Remember, in this world, we are part of a constant spiritual battle for souls. We step into that battle when we respond with a yes to our call to mission. When we engage in the mission of evangelization, we are reaching out to help the souls of our neighbors. We are attacking the gates of hell to prevent souls from being sucked into it, helping the Lord to rescue them from the grip of sin and eternal death. The Lord has invited us to partake in this task, to reach out and kick in the gates of hell, to proclaim the Gospel both with our words and our actions, so that many may be saved. Those of us who know Jesus Christ happen to know the greatest and most significant story in history. This story isn't simply for our entertainment or to make life a little easier; it is a story that opens the way for each of us to enjoy eternal life in heaven. It is a story that everyone needs to hear and that each of us needs to share.

The Lord has invited us to partake in this task, to reach out and kick in the gates of hell, to proclaim the Gospel both with our words and our actions, so that many may be saved.

A Tireless Missionary
Saint Francis Xavier is the patron saint of missionaries in the Catholic Church. It is said that he baptized at least 30,000 souls in his work as a missionary — not a bad way to engage in the mission of the Church.

Francis was from a well-to-do family in Navarre. As a young man, he went to Paris to study at the university. It was there that Saint Ignatius befriended him and brought him into a small fraternity of men who would become the Society of Jesus in 1540. Their dream was to go to the Holy Land and convert all the nonbelievers to Christianity. Instead, Ignatius sent Francis to India. Francis began his travels on his thirty-fifth birthday, burning with a great love of Jesus Christ and a great love of souls. Ignatius's last words to Francis before he left were "Go set all on fire!" This command became the center of Francis's life, which, sadly, lasted only eleven more years. In his own words, we see his love of souls and hear a piercing challenge to mission that should rock each of us to the core:

> Many, many people hereabouts are not becoming Christians for one reason: there is nobody to make them Christians. Again and again I have thought of going round the universities of Europe, especially Paris, and everywhere crying out like a madman. Riveting the attention of those with more learning than charity: What a tragedy: how many souls are being shut out of heaven and falling into hell, thanks to you! I wish they would work as hard at this as they do at their books, and so settle their account with God for their learning and the talents entrusted to them.[47]

His words remind me of the words of Jesus: "The harvest is plentiful, but the laborers are few; pray therefore the Lord of the harvest to send out laborers into his harvest" (Mt 9:37–38).

Francis worked tirelessly to build up the Church in India, especially among the Portuguese who came to colonize that land. He built forty churches in about three years before heading to the Maluku Islands and meeting a young Japanese man who told him all about Japan. In 1549, Francis was finally able to travel to Japan, where it was illegal to convert to Christianity. That didn't stop him from engaging in mission. His efforts were not immediately fruitful and eventually were met with a great persecution. From there, Francis set sail for China, a trip that would be his last. He reached an island off the coast of China and fell ill with a fever. This illness, an internal burning, was perhaps fitting for a man who sought with his whole being to set the world on fire for Jesus Christ. He died on December 3, 1552, and is heralded as one of the greatest missionaries, second only to Saint Paul.

Francis traveled from France to India and then to Japan and China in spite of the dangers and difficulties of travel in the sixteenth century. By comparison, we can certainly bear the inconvenience of engaging in evangelization for an hour or responding to the Holy Spirit's prompting to talk to the guy sitting next to us on the plane. Saint Francis's life calls to us as a challenge to elevate our involvement in the mission of evangelization, the mission of the Church. I think it is worth repeating his words for each of us to hear again: "Many, many people hereabouts are not becoming Christians for one reason: there is nobody to make them Christians."

•••

Stepping into mission is our best chance to transform the public square. The culture is shaped by people willing to partake in its shaping, and it is up to us to ensure that Christ has a foothold there. We, as men, must proclaim Jesus and all we hold dear as his disciples and allow those truths to shape all of reality. The truths we believe are not truths just for us; they are the truths of existence. And so, without forcing people to believe, we must seek to shape society by truths that are real; not your truth and my truth and their truth and anyone's truth, but *the* Truth.

Our society allowed men to be property as slaves until enough brave souls stepped forth to change it. Our society allowed only white men to vote until brave men and women fought for equality. Our society kills babies in the womb, promotes the breakdown of the family, pushes same-sex marriage, and even seeks to impose widespread acceptance of transgender ideology. This is not the will of our heavenly Father, who loves us tenderly. This is not the plan that will allow us to flourish. This culture of death can lead only to despair and destruction. Who will reshape it, if not us? Who will step in and alter the course of our culture toward reality? Who will guard and protect truth? We all need to engage, in whatever way we are able. It will make a far-reaching difference in the course of history. Our faith is not private, even if it is personal. It is meant to be shared at every moment with every soul. As we step out in the world, seeking to guard and protect it, may our proclamation of the Gospel always be evident. In this way, we advance well in the task to *shamar* souls.

Our faith is not private, even if it is personal. It is meant to be shared at every moment with every soul.

Pursuing mission can be one of the most uncomfortable things we do. As Catholics, we especially seem to become queasy at the thought of evangelization. Here are some concepts and ideas to reflect upon, as well as a few tips to start sharing the Gospel yourself:

- Evangelization does not mean that you must walk door to door or stand on a park bench and preach (although it could).
- Evangelization includes the initial proclamation of the Gospel, but it doesn't end until one is living in the fullness of the sacramental life in the Catholic Church and has also become an evangelist.
- Who are three or four men in your life you could begin to share Jesus with? How can you seek to develop a genuine friendship with these men? Forming genuine friendships is the most effective way to lead people to Jesus.
- We should strive first to be living witnesses to Jesus, yet the Gospel also needs to be spoken. Reflect on Romans 10:13–15: "'Everyone who calls upon the name of the Lord will be saved.' But how are men to call upon him in whom they have not believed? And how are they to believe in him of whom they have never heard? And how are they to hear without a preacher? And how can men preach unless they are sent? As it is written, 'How beautiful are the feet of those who preach good news!'"

CHAPTER 9
Reflect the Ultimate — Charity

He who does not love does not know God; for God is love.
1 John 4:8

•••

Do not forget that true love sets no conditions. It does not calculate or complain, but simply loves.
Pope Saint John Paul II

In every room of our house (except the bathrooms, I think), we have an image of a man being murdered. My family chooses to keep this image of Jesus Christ on the cross present throughout our home to remind us of the truth that we are loved immensely. It is difficult to grasp fully the sacrifice of God on the cross, but the crucifix reminds us of the brutality, vulnerability, as well as the sheer courage and dedication of Jesus Christ. Yet perhaps the hardest truth staring at us from the crucifix is the profoundness of God's love for us — a love we are called to imitate. "Greater love has no man than this, that a man lay down his life for his friends" (Jn 15:13).

Thankfully, this love we're called to live has a face — it is Jesus. In the Gospels, we hear of moments when Jesus was angry, protective, tender, and even sad to the point of tears. He was not a stoic, heartless man. Yet we understand his love best when we see that he went so far as to die because of it. Seeing the example of someone laying his life down is perhaps the easiest way for us as men to understand what love looks like. Today, seeing images of first responders and soldiers can help with this as well.

Yet the very notion of love seems to be lost among men in our modern culture. Many men today are distant, reticent, and emotionally neutered. Or, on the other extreme, some men have become overly sentimental or permissive concerning the desires of the people in their lives, no matter how harmful or twisted those desires might be. Strength has become indifference. Tenderness is now relativism. But real love has an intensity, and this love is fundamental to understanding why our duty to *shamar* is so significant. As I mentioned in the beginning of this book, love is our ultimate aim as human beings. We, as men, live within that goal when we adequately seek to *shamar*.

Love is our ultimate aim as human beings.

A Witness to Love

On April 8, 2005, I joined millions of people around the world to watch the funeral of John Paul II. I was in Australia at the time, but I watched on television. Rome was flooded with over a million pilgrims who came to pray for a man most of them had never met. Thousands overflowed from St. Peter's Square for the funeral Mass of one of the greatest figures of the twentieth century.

Gathered together for the occasion were over 200 of the world's dignitaries. Snipers were set out across Vatican City, Rome's airport was shut down, military ships stood off the coast of Italy, fighter planes were prepared for a defensive stand, and authorities had special forces sweeping the Tiber River for explosives. Even more impressive was the fact that known political enemies were sitting *two seats* apart from one another, perhaps for the only time in history. Presidents, prime ministers, princes, and kings, the most powerful on the face of the earth, came to pay their respects to John Paul II. How is it that the death of a man who stood directly counter to much of world opinion, whose ideals and beliefs challenged and were in return challenged by so many in politics and the media, brought the world to a standstill?

The answer is simple: John Paul II was a witness. He taught the world about the primacy of love through the very life he lived. He called out to the truth of love in our lives. He awoke the longing in every soul, the longing that God gives to each of us, to love and be loved. He was, in a way that words fail to capture, a living witness to something beyond this world. As the Vicar of Christ, he was a world leader, but he was also something more. He was a sign of hope — a hope for something greater than anything this world has to offer, the promise of a joy that never ends. In a world where so many find themselves lost and confused about the meaning of life, John Paul II pointed to a destiny that promised the fulfillment of our deepest longings. He was the face of Jesus Christ to the world — and that face is love.

Only in God do we find rest; only in Jesus Christ do we find the answer to the question of human life. That is why an estimated two billion people watched the funeral Mass of this holy man, removing the world's most powerful leaders from the center of attention for one day. It also explains why John Paul II is so dearly missed by those who were alive before he passed. He reminded all of us of our purpose in life and the one thing that can satisfy our deepest longing: the love of the Divine Trinity — Father, Son and Holy Spirit.[48] In his own words, "Man cannot live without love. He remains a being that is incomprehensible for himself, his life is senseless, if love is not revealed to him, if he does not encounter love, if he does not experience it and make it his own, if he does not participate intimately in it."[49]

Saint John Paul II had a vision of greatness that extended beyond this world. He also had the freedom to pursue it. He was free to love, to give, and to die, and he responded to the call of discipleship with amazing courage and dedication.

•••

In talking about the witness of love that John Paul II gave so well, we can easily forget how demanding this is. Sometimes when we hear of love, we think of a chick flick, or heart-shaped chocolates on Valentine's Day, or maybe even chubby little angels. That is not the love a man is called to give. A man is designed to initiate, to stand in the gap, to guard the true, the good, and the beautiful. This love will often require extreme sacrifice. This is one of the reasons I am so grateful for my days playing competitive sports. So often I was willing to throw my body around, to sacrifice aspects of myself in the hope of helping my team win. These moments have brought me closer to the capacity of love as a man — to give and not to count the cost, to risk everything for the good of another.

The love of a man doesn't drive him to cower in fear. It allows him to act in the freedom he was designed for — to guard and keep what has been entrusted to him, even to the point of death. That is why our call as men to guard and protect is such a key insight into living *masculine* love. It engages, initiates, and draws others to truth in love. When we *shamar*, we are intentionally living out a massive aspect of the love we are called to give. We do this when we speak into the culture and engage as much as we are able to in public policy. We do this when we lead our families in prayer and living a sacramental life, setting an example in our own practice. We do this when we take responsibility to care for the health of our home (physically,

The love of a man doesn't drive him to cower in fear. It allows him to act in the freedom he was designed for.

spiritually, and emotionally) rather than just relegate it to our wives or, if single, assume that a roommate will handle it. We do this when we imitate Jesus Christ and seek in all things to bring him glory. This takes intentionality in all that we do. We need to reengage. We need to start loving again.

In our families, this means protecting our wives and children from things that could harm them, not just physically, but spiritually as well. We should lead our families to Sunday Mass. We should be aware of what our children are reading and watching, and whom they spend time with, especially on social media. We need to call our friends to a higher standard — and we should go out of our way to seek out and cultivate male friendships of real depth.

Everything we do should be done in love. The themes presented in this book and the eight saints put forward as examples all point to this reality. It all culminates in love. We're called to live our lives, as they did, for the good of others.

And we do it one step at a time, each in our own unique way. How can we shake off the daze that we often find ourselves in and begin again? Love is a choice that we need to make each moment of the day. As we pursue freedom, that choice becomes easier, strengthened by God's grace.

For example: What is an area in the culture where you might develop a greater expertise and deeper involvement? What is one prayer you can begin to say with your family (daily or once a week)? How can you make Sunday Mass, or even daily Mass, a part of your family's culture? What about confession? How can you become more invested in the lives of your children and their world (as a father, not a peer)? Who are a few guys you can begin to meet with regularly to study Scripture or to share more of your hopes, struggles, and aspirations so you can help one another grow as men of God? What activity will help these friendships start to go deeper?

The world is in desperate need of genuine heroes, not Spiderman or Captain America. It needs real men who are willing to stand for the Truth in everyday life, who will guide others to it, and who are ready to die for it so that love can be known and experienced by all. That is our task.

That is our calling.

We are those men.

Notes

1. Archbishop Charles Chaput, "Things Worth Dying For: The Nature of a Life Worth Living," *Public Discourse*, October 13, 2019, accessed January 8, 2020, https://www .thepublicdiscourse.com/2019/10/57682/.

2. In 2017, 56.7 percent of the undergraduate population was female. Compare this with 1990, when it was 54.5 percent, and with 1980, when it was 51.4 percent. See National Center for Education Statistics, *Digest of Education Statistics*, table 303.10, accessed January 25, 2020, https://nces .ed.gov/programs/digest/d18/tables/dt18_303.10.asp.

3. According to MarketingCharts.com in 2017, the percentage of older millennials (25 to 34) living in their parents' homes remains at an all-time survey high, just above 16 percent. That's up from a low of 10.2 percent in 2003. Additionally, men ages 25 to 34 are 57 percent more likely than women ages 25 to 34 to be living in their parents' homes (19.6 percent and 12.5 percent, respectively). See "The Majority of 18-23-Year-Olds Live in Their Parents' Home, as Do 1 in 6 Older Millennials," MarketingCharts, December 4, 2017, accessed January 22, 2020, https://www .marketingcharts.com/demographics-and-audiences-81471.

4. Jeff A. Benner, "Keep," Ancient Hebrew Research Center, accessed January 22, 2020, https://www.ancient-hebrew

.org/definition/keep.htm.

5. Brian Pizzalato, "Adam: High Priest of Humanity," Catholic News Agency, accessed January 22, 2020, https://www.catholicnewsagency.com/resources/sacraments/holy-orders/adam-high-priest-of-humanity. See also the Catholic Study Bible app by Ignatius Press and the Augustine Institute, note on Genesis 2:15.

6. Br. Francis Mary, ed., *Padre Pio, the Wonder Worker* (San Francisco: Ignatius Press, 1999), 9–10.

7. Patricia Treece, *Quiet Moments with Padre Pio: 120 Daily Readings* (Ann Arbor, MI: Servant Publications, 1999), no. 88.

8. Staretz Nicodemus, foreword to *Unseen Warfare* (New York: St. Vladimir's Seminary Press, 1997), 15.

9. Dom Lorenzo Scupoli, *The Spiritual Combat* (Rockford, IL: TAN Publishers, 1945), 45.

10. National Coalition against Domestic Violence, "Domestic Violence," accessed January 22, 2020, https://assets.speakcdn.com/assets/2497/domestic_violence2.pdf.

11. See United States Office on Drugs and Crime, "Worldwide Statistics," linked to in Jarryd Bartle, "The Scientific Reasons Why Men Are More Violent Than Women," *New York Post*, January 16, 2019, accessed January 22, 2020, https://nypost.com/2019/01/16/the-scientific-reasons-why-men-are-more-violent-than-women/.

12. National Coalition against Domestic Violence, "Statistics," accessed January 22, 2020, https://www.ncadv.org/statistics.

13. James B. Stenson, *Successful Fathers: The Subtle but Powerful Ways Fathers Mold Their Children's Characters* (Princeton: Scepter Publishers, 2001), 60–61. Stenson also writes about how most of the time children are witnessing

their fathers when they are at home after work, exhausted and in leisure mode. He then writes on page 34, "If a father spent much time talking with his children about his life outside their experience (of dad in leisure mode) — that is, his job and his personal history, his concerns and worries, his opinions and convictions — he could compensate considerably for his absence during most of the children's waking hours. The children would learn at least something about his character. Such father-children discussion was common until the invention of television. ... Talk of any sort between fathers and children frequently totals less than 20 minutes a day. Really serious conversations, by which children learn about Dad's life and character, is extremely rare."

14. Barna, *The Porn Phenomenon: The Impact of Pornography on the Digital Age* (Ventura, CA: Barna Resources and Josh McDowell Ministry, 2016), 32.

15. Ibid., 142.

16. Ibid.

17. Ibid., 91.

18. "The purpose and goal of *temperantia* is man's inner order, from which alone this 'serenity of spirit' can flow forth. 'Temperance' signifies the realizing of this order within oneself." Josef Pieper, *The Four Cardinal Virtues* (South Bend, IN: Notre Dame Press, 1966), 147.

19. John A. O'Brien, *The First Martyrs of North America: The Story of the Eight Jesuit Martyrs* (South Bend, IN: University of Notre Dame Press, 1960), 110.

20. Ibid., 119.

21. Ibid., 122–23.

22. Ibid., 172.

23. Benedict XVI, *Deus Caritas Est*, accessed January 22,

2020, Vatican.va, par. 6.

24. See John Robinson, *Spiritual Combat, Revisited* (San Francisco: Ignatius Press, 2003), 127–38.

25. Leonard Sax, *Boys Adrift* (New York: Basic Books, 2016), 7.

26. Ibid.

27. Antonio Ricciardi, *Saint Maximilian Kolbe* (Boston: Daughters of St. Paul, 1982), 19.

28. "It is related that one day Father Maximilian was seen attentively studying a map of the world, calculating the distances from place to place. Then after voicing a few reflections on the customs and religions of those who populated the various continents, in an inspired manner he exclaimed: 'The Knights of the Immaculata must have missions! In spite of all the differences, we must have faith in the Immaculata. For this purpose, she will send us many vocations.'" Ibid., 125.

29. Ibid., 163.

30. Ibid., 173.

31. Ibid., 223.

32. Helene Mongin, *The Extraordinary Parents of St. Thérèse of Lisieux* (Huntington, IN: Our Sunday Visitor, 2015), 21–22.

33. Ibid., 147.

34. Ibid.

35. Celine Martin, *The Father of the Little Flower* (Charlotte, NC: Tan Books, 2005), 79.

36. Ibid.

37. Mongin, *Extraordinary Parents*, 150.

38. Martin, *Father of the Little Flower*, 98.

39. Margaret and Matthew Bunson, *Apostle of the Exiled: St. Damien of Molokai* (Huntington, IN: Our Sunday Visi-

tor, 2009), 111.

40. Ibid., 117.

41. Ibid., 127.

42. Ibid., 139.

43. Saint Alphonsus de Liguori, *Uniformity with God's Will* (Charlotte, NC: Tan Books), 17.

44. John Paul II, *Redemptoris Custos*, accessed January 22, 2020, Vatican.va, par. 4.

45. Ignatius of Loyola, *Spiritual Exercises*, "Principle and Foundation," no. 23.

46. See Paul VI, *Evangelii Nuntiandi*, accessed January 22, 2020, Vatican.va, par. 14.

47. Office of Readings, December 3.

48. "Being Christian is not the result of an ethical choice or a lofty idea, but the encounter with an event, a person, which gives life a new horizon and a decisive direction." Benedict XVI, *Deus Caritas Est*, par. 1.

49. John Paul II, *Redemptor Hominis*, accessed January 22, 2020, Vatican.va, par. 10.

About the Author

THOMAS WURTZ is a husband and father of five. He has a bachelor's degree from Benedictine College and a master's degree from the Augustine Institute. He started working as a lay missionary with the Fellowship of Catholic University Students (FOCUS) in 2001, founded its outreach to athletes (Varsity Catholic) in 2007, and, in 2016, launched its effort to help men find freedom from pornography struggles. He has also helped lead and design FOCUS's men's formation for over a decade. He is the author of *Compete Inside: 100 Reflections to Help You Become the Complete Athlete* and was selected as a delegate to the inaugural Sport at the Service of Humanity Conference, hosted by the Pontifical Council of Culture in the Vatican.

What makes a man?

This is a question many men
in our society today do not feel
equipped to answer, because they
were never initiated into manhood
themselves. They do not know how
to pass on authentic manliness
to their sons, so boys get stuck in
unending adolescence. Everyone
suffers from the resulting crisis of
male immaturity, and we see its
effects everywhere in our society.

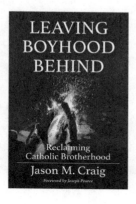

Leaving Boyhood Behind shows how we can actually
do something to address this crisis. Author Jason Craig,
cofounder of Fraternus, a Catholic mentoring program for
boys, walks through each stage of initiation into manhood,
helping readers understand:

- What rites of passage are and why they are
  necessary for men
- Christ's own rites of passage and initiation
- What it means for a young man to put away
  childhood
- The importance of belonging vs. isolation in the
  life of men
- The important role both mothers and fathers place
  in initiation
- Discipline and the masculine identity
- Living the ultimate rite of passage, and much more

"This book is an invaluable resource for all Catholics
who care about the intellectual, physical, and spiritual
development of the next generation of men." — Deacon
Harold Burke-Sivers, author of *Behold the Man: A Catholic
Vision of Male Spirituality*